Bristol Rovers Greats

Bristol Rovers
Greats

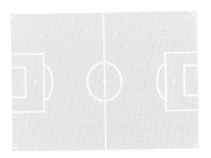

Ivan Ponting

Richard Jones

redcliffe

In association with the

EVENING POST

Statistical Note

The main dates accompanying the profiles refer to the seasons in which each player appeared in the Rovers first team, not when he joined and left the club. In the brief statistical resumé at the end of each profile, goals and appearances under the heading 'Others' are in respect of matches in the Football League promotion play-offs, Watney Cup, Anglo-Scottish Cup, Anglo-Italian Cup, Associate Members' Cup, Freight Rover Trophy, Sherpa Van Trophy, Leyland Daf Cup, Zenith Data Systems Cup, Autoglass Trophy, Auto Windscreens Shield and the LDV Vans Trophy. The figures under the heading 'Other Clubs' includes League appearances and goals only. Substitute appearances are in brackets. Figures relating to the League Cup also refer to its successors, the Milk Cup, the Littlewoods Cup, the Rumbelows Cup, the Coca-Cola Cup, the Worthington Cup and the Carling Cup. Figures in the 'On The Bench' section which begins on page 150 refer to all first-class games for the club. All records are complete to the end of the 2004/05 season.

First published by Redcliffe Press Ltd., in 1990
This new and enlarged edition published in 2005 by Redcliffe Press Ltd., 81g Pembroke Road, Bristol BS8 3EA

© Ivan Ponting and Richard Jones

ISBN 1 904537 34 0

British Library Cataloguing-in-Publication Data
A catalogue record for this book is available from the British Library

DESIGNED BY STEPHEN MORRIS COMMUNICATIONS, SMC@FREEUK.COM
PRINTED AND BOUND IN MALTA BY GUTENBERG PRESS LTD

Contents

Introduction

LET'S BE HONEST. Watching Bristol Rovers in the new millennium has been, for the most part, a grisly business, but it has not always been like that.

As a soccer-mad youngster in the late 1950s and early 1960s, I made a belated but infinitely satisfying discovery: Manchester United were not the only team in the world worth watching. I was convinced by the silver tongues of Jeff Ford, a sporting stalwart in my home village of Chewton Mendip, and his equally persuasive brother Melv, that Eastville and Ashton Gate were the places to go.

Particularly in those days when the M5 and M6 were still green fields, the Bristol grounds were conveniently accessible destinations compared to Old Trafford, and I became a regular follower of both the Pirates and the Robins.

It was Jeff – to whom I shall be forever grateful – who would take me to Eastville, never failing to impress on me the finer points of the game as practised by Messrs Bradford and Biggs, and I was captivated by the unique atmosphere of the place. It was warm and homely, right down to the smell from the nearby gas-holder, yet it was also the stage for thrilling deeds by some of soccer's most appealing characters.

In the first edition of this book, which was published in 1990, I attempted to capture the essence of the men who made the biggest impact on me down the years, as well as heroes from before my time whose achievements had passed into Rovers' folklore. Now, 15 years on, it has been suggested to me that an update is appropriate and so, having not been as regular a visitor to The Memorial Stadium as I would have liked, I have enlisted the aid of experienced journalist and lifelong Gashead Richard Jones to supply a series of new profiles on leading players of recent times.

In our quest for information to back up our own observations, we have spoken with many former players, who have been unfailingly generous with their time and enthusiasm, as well as fans whose comprehensive memories have proved invaluable.

Last time I was limited by considerations of space to profiles of 50 post-war Pirates; this time we have added 20 more, though doubtless there will be readers who disagree with some of our final selections. But football remains, after all, a game of opinions, and herein are Richard's and mine. In an effort to widen the scope, we have included at the back an extended section containing photographs of 48 players who just missed out, though even that inevitably omits some splendid performers, and to them we apologise.

At the time of the first edition I wrote that recent triumphs by Gerry Francis's invigorating team had brought new life to one of the West Country's most beloved sporting institutions, and that the future, while challenging, was full of hope. As it turned out, 'challenging' was a chronic understatement. Still, there have been some peaks among the troughs, and certainly Rovers have nurtured some high-quality players, notably a succession of strikers who have gone on to prove their worth at higher levels.

In football there is always another day, another season, and the Pirates have laudably ambitious plans for the rest of the decade and beyond. So let's hope that the third edition of Bristol Rovers Greats, scheduled loosely (and optimistically) for the year 2020, will carry tributes to fresh heroes of genuine stature, men fit to rank alongside the revered giants of the past.

Ivan Ponting, September 2005

Acknowledgements

FROM IVAN PONTING
Pat, Rosie and Joe Ponting for unending patience and support; Stephen Morris for revolutionising the design; Clara Sansom for enlightened editorship; Andy Cowie of Colorsport for never being beaten; Alfie Biggs for his foreword and his 197 goals; Chris Bartlett, John England and Rob Stokes of the *Evening Post*; John Sansom.

FROM RICHARD JONES
Maggie, Caitlin and Mena Telfer, Jamie Shore, Carl Saunders, Phil Purnell, Andy Tillson, Roy Dolling, Brian Parkin, Dave Phillips, Campbell Stevenson, Chris Swift, Geraint Williams.

FURTHER ACKNOWLEDGEMENTS FROM THE FIRST BOOK
Peter Aitken; Doug Baker; George Baker; Bob Boyd; Alec Briggs; Bobby Campbell; Ken Clarke; Joe Davis; Keith Fear; Jeff Ford; Lucy Graham; John Hudson; Harold Jarman; Bobby Jones; Lindsay Parsons; Robin Perry; Jackie Pitt; Frankie Prince; Phil Roberts; Steve Small; Gerry Brooke and the staff of the *Evening Post* library; all at Colorsport.

Foreword

BRISTOL ROVERS MEAN MORE TO ME THAN WORDS CAN SAY. They were the dominant influence on my footballing career and I love the club dearly. Even today, having retired to Poole, there is nothing I enjoy more than a visit to the Memorial Ground to watch a match and catch up with friends. But, if I'm honest, nothing compares to the glorious days at dear old Eastville.

Playing for Rovers in the 1950s and 1960s was like living a dream for me, and Eastville seemed like some sort of paradise. The ground had a fantastic atmosphere all of its own, what with the greyhound track and the flowerbeds behind the goals. As for the famous smell of gas, it didn't bother us in the least because we were used to it. Maybe it put off the opposition a little, though, perhaps carrying a whiff of intimidation, proclaiming 'This is Eastville!'

Rovers was always such a homely club, with a friendlier feel than any other I encountered. There were no delusions of grandeur, right from the board of directors all the way down to the tea-ladies. Everyone was approachable and pulling in the same direction.

When I got into the side in 1953, nine of the lads were Bristolians. It really was the local club and the fans picked up on that. Once I had signed on at Eastville I never had a moment's regret about missing out at City, who I had followed as a boy but who then rejected me in my teens. Given roughly equal standing in the League table, I believe Rovers would always have the bigger and more vociferous following of the two Bristol clubs, such is the passion and loyalty of their supporters.

I felt privileged to become part of an outstanding side, which finished in the top half of the old Second Division in all of my first seven seasons in professional football. Twice we came sixth, and in 1955/56 we were only four points short of winning promotion to the First Division. I'm certain we would have made it if we hadn't lost Geoff Bradford, our magnificent centre-forward, to a serious injury in the January. Even without Geoff we went close, only to be beaten in our last couple of games by Leeds and Liverpool, which was a mighty disappointment.

Of course, the highlight of that season was our remarkable home victory over Manchester United in the FA Cup, arguably the most memorable triumph in Bristol Rovers' entire history. This was not any old United team but the brilliant Busby Babes, two years before they were decimated in the Munich air disaster.

They arrived as League leaders, and they went on to become League champions by a street, but that day at Eastville we hammered them 4-0. Perhaps United were a tad complacent, but they were parading all their stars except Duncan Edwards and, in sporting terms, it was the shock to end all shocks. I scored a couple of the goals and look back on the achievement as the pinnacle of my life in the game.

I don't think many people would argue with the assertion that Bert Tann's mid-1950s combination was the finest of all Bristol Rovers teams. Wherever you looked there were exceptional players, the likes of Harry Bamford, Ray Warren, Jackie Pitt, Peter Sampson, George Petherbridge, Peter Hooper, Josser Watling, Geoff Bradford and the rest. You couldn't fault any of them and I believe they were chronically underrated.

It's a shame that Rovers ever left Eastville and it saddens me now when I drive past on the M32 and glance across at the monstrosities that occupy the site. Even the last floodlight disappeared in 2003, taken down for safety reasons, and now all that remains is the Eastville Club, still standing rather forlornly in the corner of the car park.

But the spirit of the Rovers remains indestructible, and there have been many fine players who have worn the blue-and-white shirts, first at Twerton Park and now at The Memorial Ground. I hope that the Pirates will always prosper and that the heroes featured between the covers of this book will never be forgotten.

Alfie Biggs, Poole 2005

BORN: Cardiff, 30.6.54

ROVERS RECORD:

League: 230 (4) games, 3 goals

FA Cup: 11 games, 0 goals

League Cup: 13 games, 1 goal

Others: 6 games, 0 goals

Total: 260 (4) games, 4 goals

OTHER CLUBS:

Bristol City 80/1-81/2 (41, 1)

York City 81/2 (18, 2)

Bournemouth (non-contract) 82/3 (1, 0)

PETER AITKEN

1972/73 — 1979/80

IT WAS THE DAY Peter Aitken came of age as a player. Tranmere were the visitors to Eastville and Bristol Rovers were desperate to halt a worrying 11th-hour stutter in their Third Division promotion campaign. The 19-year-old Welshman, in the side as a surprise replacement for central defender Mike Green, went into a 50-50 challenge with Ron Yeats, the man mountain around whom Bill Shankly had built his first great Liverpool side. The two clashed thunderously, and Peter was rocked to his very foundations. Every bone in his body seemed to vibrate, but he came away with the ball – and, more significantly, a new confidence that he could compete with the toughest.

Rovers duly won that crucial encounter in the spring of 1974 and went on to reach the higher grade. Green moved on and Peter, playing with assurance alongside centre-half Stuart Taylor, completed his opening term in the Second Division as an ever-present. He had plenty to offer: good control with both feet, precise distribution and a priceless knack of reading the game that made everything he did look easy. Although he lacked that last yard of pace which would have marked him out instantly as outstanding, notable soccer judges believed he had top-flight potential.

So what stopped Peter Aitken? Initially it was a broken leg, sustained against Notting-ham Forest at Eastville in October 1975, then later he became a victim of his own versatility. Manager Don Megson often shuffled his struggling side, and the under-23 international usually found himself at full-back or in midfield. Deprived of his most effective role, he remained a solid player, but stopped making progress.

By December 1979 the Pirates' position at the foot of the table was perilous, and Peter, now skipper and restored to central defence, played a colossal part in helping caretaker boss Harold Jarman's team avoid the drop. His display in a 3-0 home trouncing of slick, experienced Chelsea was inspirational, and one of Rovers' most valuable assets seemed set for a renaissance.

But Terry Cooper took over as manager and the man known to team-mates as Charlie, after 1960s Aston Villa stalwart Charlie Aitken, joined Bristol City, whom he captained briefly before opting for the local amateur scene and a job outside soccer. Thus this likeable family man left the League with potential unfulfilled, but with the respect of many in the game who reckon he could have made it to the top.

Happily, Peter returned to the club in later years, and in 2005 he was filling the key role of Football in the Community Officer.

BORN: Glasgow, 26.1.63

ROVERS RECORD:

League: 284 (7) games, 6 goals

FA Cup: 13 games, 2 goals

League Cup: 15 games, 1 goal

Others: 24 games, 0 goals

Total: 336 (7) games, 9 goals

ROVERS HONOURS:

Third Division Championship 89/90

Leyland Daf Cup Finalist 89/90

OTHER CLUBS:

Rotherham United 81/2-82/3 (11, 0)

Pezoporikos Larnaca, Cyprus

IAN ALEXANDER

1986/87 — 1993/94

THE OPENING SHOTS for Roger Malone's HTV football show used to feature an outrageous challenge by Ian 'Jocky' Alexander on hapless Bristol City winger Dave Smith. 'That tackle looks better every week', said Malone as the viewers winced at Smith's misfortune. Glaswegian Jocky began his football career as a winger, but once he moved to right-back he appeared to lose any lingering compassion for the well-being of his former comrades on the flanks.

It would be unfair to give the impression that Alexander was a dirty player – although he was sent off six times, including three dismissals against Bristol City – but definitely he was a hard man to beat. He played with the collective determination that ran throughout the promotion-winning defence of 1990, consisting of himself, Steve Yates, Geoff Twentyman and Vaughan Jones. Yet in the dressing room Alexander was one of the most laid-back characters in the Rovers squad.

Jocky was brought to the club by Bobby Gould in 1986 and achieved greatness in the eyes of Rovers fans as one of Gerry Francis's promotion heroes. Like many of the players of this era, it seemed Alexander was motivated by the perilous position in which Rovers found themselves during their Bath exile and thrived on the remarkable support at Twerton Park, also known by Gould as 'The Azteca Stadium' and later as 'Fortress Twerton'.

The Scot had a keen sense of humour. Once at Twerton he hurled himself full-length to tip a goalbound shot around the post and immediately clutched his head in mock pain, trying to give the referee the impression that the ball had struck him in the face. Rarely has a home player received a red card for deliberate handball amid such laughter from fans, players and perhaps even officials than did the man who played more times at Twerton than any other Rovers player, with a total of 142 starts.

There were many famous Alexander moments, including a penalty save when he took over in goal from Brian Parkin against Brighton in 1991, but his most memorable performances were against Liverpool in the two fourth-round FA Cup ties of 1992. Few of the 9,484 fans at Twerton Park on that February night will forget the 90-minute battle between Alexander and Dean Saunders in the 1-1 draw which resulted in bloody noses (but hearty handshakes after the game).

In the replay at Anfield, Steve McManaman found himself up against Alexander, who marked the England international out of the game in the first half. After the interval McManaman moved to the right wing to try his luck against Steve Cross, and it's fair to speculate that if 'Jocky' had switched flanks as well then Rovers might just have clung on to their 1-0 interval lead, courtesy of a Carl Saunders long-range volley. Instead McManaman levelled the scores and set up Dean Saunders for the winner.

After ending his career with Rovers in 1994, Alexander joined Yate Town as manager, with Phil Purnell as his assistant.

BORN: Riga, Latvia, 3.4.71

ROVERS RECORD:

League: 87 (22) games, 16 goals

FA Cup: 9 (1) games, 1 goal

League Cup: 5 games, 0 goals

Others: 4 games, 2 goals

Total: 105 (23) games, 19 goals

OTHER CLUBS:

Skonto Riga, Latvia

Admira Wacker, Austria, 03/04

Latvia caps.

VITALIJS ASTAFJEVS

IT'S NOT OFTEN that an international captain turns up in the Rovers midfield and in the case of Vitalijs Astafjevs it remains something of a mystery how he came to the club and why he stayed so long. 'The Latvian', as he was referred to on the terraces, was at his peak when Ian Holloway signed him in January 2000 and he went on to captain his country at Euro 2004 in Portugal.

A handful of Rovers fans made the trip to the tournament and careful listeners to the television commentary might have heard chants of 'Ooh Arr, he's a Latvian' rising from a blue-and-white corner of the Bessa stadium in Porto as Latvia drew 0-0 with Germany to earn their first point in international finals.

The Russian-speaking Astafjevs was one of the most accomplished Rovers players of recent times and he stayed in Bristol for four seasons – the worst four seasons in Rovers' history. He was a canny midfielder with a clever pass and a strong shot, but despite these footballing qualifications, initially he had been unable to secure a work permit.

In the end Holloway's testimony to an employment tribunal made the difference and the minutes of that hearing carry great poignancy: 'Mr Astafjevs was judged to be a model professional . . . he is seen as an investment for the future and a key player for the club's promotion ambitions.'

It was the man in charge of Latvia at the time, current Yeovil manager Gary Johnson, who put Astafjevs in touch with Rovers, being keen for his internationals to play somewhere other than Skonto Riga in order to gain wider experience of European football.

Still, it must have taken all of Holloway's powers of persuasion to convince Astafjevs that joining a Second Division club was going to further his international ambitions. But The Memorial Stadium boss had a passion and a vision for Bristol Rovers, and presumably the manner in which he communicated his intentions persuaded the Latvian to sign.

The reality was that Rovers took just six points from a possible 30 in the last ten games of the season and slipped from promotion certainties to needing a win against already-relegated Cardiff City on the last day of the campaign to make the 1999/2000 play-offs. But they produced a feeble display at Ninian Park, losing 1-0 and finishing seventh in the Second Division. Of course, even worse was to come as Astafjevs spent the following term in a Rovers team relegated to the basement division for the first time in their history.

Throughout his time in Bristol Vitalijs, a private individual and a strong family man, conducted himself with dignity on and off the field. He was too good to be playing in the bottom grade for a poor Rovers side and many fans were pleased he was able to achieve a higher standard of football when he left for Admira Wacker in Austria in July 2003. It still seems bizarre that after watching him score against Cambridge in his final home game for Rovers, the next time most Gasheads saw Astafjevs he was leading out his country at Euro 2004.

HARRY BAMFORD

1946/47 — 1958/59

HARRY BAMFORD was a right-back and a gentleman, an unlikely combination in the immediate post-war years, when the majority of men in his position enjoyed a rather more brisk – some might say brutal – relationship with opposing wingers. The use of force was never Harry's way; indeed, there were times when his right-half, the more vigorous Jackie Pitt, would practically tear his hair out in frustration at Bamford's softly-softly tactics.

There was, for instance, the occasion at Exeter when Harry, trying to take the ball out of the penalty area in his customary unruffled fashion, somehow managed to walk it into his own net; it is an incident which Jackie recalled later with a grin, but it provoked a rather more earthy reaction at the time.

Almost invariably, Harry's game was devastatingly effective, and his elegant methods earned the respect of team-mates and the adulation of supporters. He was a perfectionist who, once in possession of the ball, liked to use it constructively. Some reckoned he practised his skills by dribbling around his beloved racing pigeons, but more likely the technique was a throwback to pre-war days as an amateur inside-forward with Bristol City.

He linked fluently with Pitt and right-winger George Petherbridge, and many attacks originated from his delicate touches.

Remarkably, in view of the number of players given their chance before and after Alf Ramsey's lengthy tenure in the England side, his only representative recognition was a tour of Australia with the FA.

Harry's almost saintly footballing reputation was reflected in his behaviour off the field. He was big and strong without being a bully, a fitness fanatic, an impeccable sportsman, an inspiration to Rovers' youngsters and a devoted family man. It might be supposed that such a catalogue of qualities would have added up to an insufferably self-righteous type whom most normal, red-blooded individuals would feel justified in punching on the nose. Not a bit of it; Harry was one of the lads, a much loved member of the team in every respect.

His premature death in a motorcycle accident in Clifton in the autumn of 1958 dismayed the West's sporting public. More than 35,000 packed Eastville when a combined Rovers and City side played Arsenal in a testimonial for his wife and family. Though 38 years old when he was killed, he was performing as well as ever, and might have carried on for several more seasons. When Harry Bamford was taken from them, the Rovers were left with a void it was impossible to fill.

BORN: Bristol, 8.2.20

DIED: Bristol, 31.10.58

ROVERS RECORD:

League: 486 games, 5 goals

FA Cup: 38 games, 0 goals

Total: 524 games, 5 goals

ROVERS HONOURS:

Third Division South Championship 52/3

BRUCE BANNISTER

1971/72 — 1976/77

IF THEY HANDED OUT trophies for self-confidence, then Bruce Bannister wouldn't get into his house for silverware. The chirpy little Yorkshireman, immortalised in Rovers' folklore as the second half of the prolific 'Smash and Grab' goal-scoring partnership with Alan Warboys, was one of the most positive dressing-room influences on the side that won promotion to the Second Division in 1973/74.

Bruce, recalled with affection by former team-mates as the man who was never wrong, had a word for everyone and an answer to everything. When Bill Dodgin paid Bradford City £23,000 for his signature in November 1971, he breezed into Eastville and immediately lit up the place with his irrepressible approach.

The 5ft 7½in striker's football was an extension of his personality. His game boasted the swagger of a born entertainer, and the fans loved him for it. They were also rather fond of his goals, which he scored with gratifying regularity, the product of swift reflexes, courage, and often sheer cheek.

'BB' was a natural predator, a snapper-up of unconsidered trifles in the six-yard area, who was continually looking for knock-downs by colleagues and rebounds from defenders, although undeniably he did his fair share of hard graft. He roamed the width of the pitch, employing his strength and chunky build to hold the ball before laying it off deftly, often taking fearful punishment from towering defenders in the process. Adept at turning in tight spaces and surprising opponents with sudden blind-side runs, Bruce was dangerous in the air for a short man and was blessed with adequate, if hardly adhesive, ball control.

He formed tolerably effective strike-forces with Robin Stubbs, John Rudge and Sandy Allan, but it wasn't until the arrival of the strapping Warboys that Bannister was seen at his lethal peak. Together they spearheaded the promotion campaign, their styles complementary, with Bruce perhaps the more single-minded in front of goal.

The duo didn't prosper in the Second Division, and was split when 'Grab', who always found time to help youngsters and was a dedicated worker for the players' union, joined Plymouth in 1976. After another liaison with Alan at Hull he went into business, predictably succeeding with a sports equipment firm in his native county.

Bruce Bannister always thought he should be in the top flight, but never reached it; probably he would say that Division One's loss was greater than his own.

BORN: Bradford, Yorkshire, 14.4.47

ROVERS RECORD:

League: 202 (4) games, 80 goals

FA Cup: 13 (2) games, 5 goals

League Cup: 17 games, 5 goals

Others: 5 games, 3 goals

Total: 237 (6) games, 93 goals

ROVERS HONOURS:

Promotion from Third Division 73/4

Watney Cup 72/3

OTHER CLUBS:

Bradford City 65/6-71/2 (208, 60)

Plymouth Argyle 76/7 (24, 2)

Hull City 77/8-79/80 (85, 20)

BORN: Bristol, 12.9.59

DIED: Bristol, 14.8.84

ROVERS RECORD:

League: 119 (9) games, 18 goals

FA Cup: 7 (1) games, 2 goals

League Cup: 12 games, 3 goals

Others: 3 games, 0 goals

Total: 141 (10) games, 23 goals

MIKE BARRETT

1979/80 — 1983/84

TO WATCH MIKE BARRETT express himself on a football pitch was to witness a brilliant but unpredictable artist at his canvas. On his day he could conjure up sublime images to take the breath away; on others he might tantalise, merely hinting at the depth of his talents, but one thing was sure. It was always worth taking a look, just in case.

Mike was a winger with ability to burn. Naturally left-sided, though he could also play on the right, he had a round-shouldered, deceptively ungainly build and was hardly the fleetest of flankmen. His special skill, the natural variety that no amount of coaching could instil, had little to do with pace and a lot to do with a mesmeric body-swerve calculated to turn defenders into gibbering wrecks. Mike seemed to drift by his opponents, almost daring them to claim the ball, then stretching out a long leg to touch it past them at the last moment.

Having infiltrated the defence, he might float a tempting cross towards the likes of Archie Stephens or Paul Randall, or try for goal himself. He possessed a powerful shot but sometimes tended to loft the ball, frustratingly, from dangerous positions, and he was in his element when making chances rather than taking them.

Surprisingly for such a gifted player, Mike was a late starter in the professional game. After a spell at Ashton Gate as a youngster, he made a name in the local leagues before being spotted by Harold Jarman. Then 19, he had recently been offered a trial by Manchester United and had taken the bold step of giving up his job to get fit for it. Harold invited him to do his training at Eastville, and he ended up as a Pirate.

Barrett's senior breakthrough came in the spring of 1980, and initial impressions were of thrilling virtuosity marred by bouts of indifferent form. One remarkable early display, just eight months after his debut, came in the FA Cup at Deepdale, when he lacerated the Preston defence, inspiring his side to a 4-0 lead; Rovers hung on to win 4-3.

By 1983/84 he was at last attaining consistency, and looked to be the player around whom manager David Williams might mould a promotion side. But he struggled to keep up with his team-mates in pre-season training, entered hospital for tests, and within weeks had died of cancer at the age of 24.

Mike Barrett was a modest, likeable young man who was overjoyed to be making his living at the game he loved. He seemed destined for a great future, and his loss was the starkest of tragedies.

PHIL BATER

1974/75 — 1980/81 & 1983/84 — 1985/86

PHIL BATER was a born winner in a team that had to accept defeat too often for comfort. Throughout the powerhouse full-back's first and most distinguished Eastville stint, Bristol Rovers languished near the foot of the table. Yet there could hardly have been a winger in the Second Division, with the possible exception of Nottingham Forest's John Robertson, a compulsive torturer of any defender, who relished a confrontation with the resilient Welshman.

A downright refusal to be beaten was always the central tenet of Phil's footballing philosophy. That much became evident during one of his first matches for the reserves when, as the rawest of rookies, he was given the runaround by one-time Arsenal wonderboy Peter Marinello. The determination that such a chasing should never be repeated was etched vividly on his face, and he worked with fearsome dedication to see that it wasn't.

His enthusiasm in training was such that even his best friends were loth to face his whiplash tackles, and it was inevitable that such a competitive individual, also blessed with scorching pace, should achieve an early breakthrough.

When it came, as deputy for injured left-back Lindsay Parsons at home to Aston Villa in September 1974, he was pitted against former Pirate and fellow speed-merchant Ray Graydon. It was a daunting task, Ray having matured into a far more dangerous player than in his Bristol days, but it was the 18-year-old who won the day.

Lindsay was back for the next game but the versatile Phil, who was equally effective on the right flank, soon became a fixture in a team that was to rely heavily on his honest strengths. He stayed with Rovers until they were relegated in 1981, before joining Wrexham in a £50,000 deal that proved eminently more satisfactory for the sellers than the buyers. Within two years new boss David Williams had bought Bater back for just £5,000, often employing his forceful countryman's ball-winning qualities as a utility midfielder.

Phil closed his career with spells at Brentford and Cardiff before becoming a landscape gardener in Bristol. What a shame that this modest, humorous man, ever willing to turn his sharp wit against his own rather limited creative abilities, should have spent his peak years in a struggling side. No one at Eastville deserved the fruits of success more than Phil Bater.

Later Phil returned to Bristol Rovers as a coach, and served as caretaker manager either side of Ray Graydon's reign in the hot seat. Later still he went back to the soil, concentrating once more on his gardening business.

BORN: Cardiff, 26.10.55

ROVERS RECORD:

League: 301 (9) games, 3 goals

FA Cup: 22 games, 0 goals

League Cup: 14 (1) games, 0 goals

Others: 11 (1) games, 0 goals

Total: 348 (11) games, 3 goals

OTHER CLUBS:

Wrexham 81/2-82/3 (73, 1)

Brentford 86/7 (19, 2)

Cardiff City 87/8-88/9 (76, 0)

PETER BEADLE

FOR A STRIKER who seemed to enjoy scoring against Bristol City at Ashton Gate with particular relish, it seemed incongruous that Peter Beadle played close on a century of League and Cup games for the Robins later in his career.

Beadle was signed from Watford in September 1995 to replace Gareth Taylor, who had left for Crystal Palace for a club-record fee of £1.6 million. The newcomer scored 12 times in 26 games and complemented his partner, Marcus Stewart, who enjoyed his finest season in front of goal with 21 strikes.

Those impressive tallies justified manager John Ward's acquisition of the burly Londoner so that Stewart would have a much-needed target man to play alongside, following the departures of Devon White and John Taylor in recent seasons.

But there was much more to Beadle's game than supporting his partner, as Rovers fans discovered on a famous night at Ashton Gate in January 1996. It was the first time Rovers had played City in the League for three seasons, and at their previous meeting City fans had gloated when their team's 2-1 victory had helped to relegate Rovers to the Second Division. That evening sounds of 'Goodbye Irene, Goodbye, the Gas are going down' rang around south Bristol – painful listening for all those of the blue-and-white persuasion.

Not surprisingly the atmosphere at Ashton Gate three years later was hostile as newly-demoted City looked to establish themselves as Bristol's better team. But Beadle seized the opportunity to silence the Robins' faithful with two second-half goals, the first a tap-in from Andy Gurney's cross, the second a left-foot drive from the edge of the box that will live long in the memory.

The following season Beadle slid home a 90th-minute equaliser to earn Rovers a 1-1 draw and become the first Rovers player to score three League goals at Ashton Gate since Dai Ward in the 1950s.

The delight in The Memorial Stadium when Peter scored his first League hat-trick in a ten-minute blitz against Bury (the third came from another thumping effort from well outside the area) wasn't just for the victory but for a deserved milestone in the career of a loyal servant.

Beadle was never the most flamboyant or prolific marksman and he would often act as provider rather than finisher. It was from this deep role that he produced one of his finest moments, when he took possession in the centre-circle and powered through the Wisbech defence to score in an FA Cup tie in the Fens in December 1997.

Probably he deserved more goals than he scored for Rovers, but also he made a key contribution as a steadying influence in the difficult days after the departure of Gerry Francis and his promotion-winning heroes. That role was typified when he grabbed an Eastertime winner against Peterborough at London Road to lift Rovers out of the 1997 relegation battle.

Like any striker Peter Beadle missed opportunities, but he will always be remembered affectionately by Rovers fans for that glorious rash of derby goals at Ashton Gate.

BORN: Lambeth, London, 13.5.72

ROVERS RECORD:

League: 98 (11) games, 39 goals

FA Cup: 5 games, 2 goals

League Cup: 2 (1) games, 0 goals

Others: 7 (1) games, 1 goal

Total: 112 (13) games, 42 goals

OTHER CLUBS:

Gillingham 88/9-91/2 (67, 14)

Tottenham Hotspur 92/3 (0, 0)

Bournemouth on loan 92/3 (9, 2)

Southend United on loan 93/4 (8, 1)

Watford 94/5-95/6 (23, 1)

Port Vale 98/9 (23, 6)

Notts County 98/9-99/00 (22, 3)

Bristol City 99/00-02/03 (82, 14)

Brentford 03/04 (1, 0)

ALFIE BIGGS

NOTHING BUT LACK OF AMBITION kept Alfie Biggs from playing for England – and that's not just the blue-and-white tinted view of one who watched his exploits from the terraces with the goggle-eyed awe and affection of a schoolboy.

Jimmy Milne, the Preston boss who took him to Deepdale and then sent him back to Eastville after 15 months because he was pining for the West Country, described Alfie as the best player he had ever bought; Stan Cullis of the mighty Wolves called North End's Biggs deal the coup of the season; and Bert Tann, who sold the blond Bristolian because Rovers needed the cash, yet seemed vastly relieved to bring him home, saw Alfie as one of the best three centre-forwards in the land.

In terms of natural all-round ability, probably there has never been another Bristol man like him. Alfie had the lot: a fine touch with both feet, power and control in the air and a fierce shot. He was bountifully endowed with strength, courage and pace, he possessed the vision of a play-maker and adopted an unusually unselfish approach for such a prolific goal-scorer. The Biggs cocktail was enough to make any manager drool – but there was, of course, a catch.

Alfie was easy-going, what it is now fashionable to call laid back. Not for him the pressurised life of a high-flier in London or the North. He was a socialiser who enjoyed a pint and a flutter, though it should be emphasised that he was never one to lead rookie team-mates astray. 'The Baron', so dubbed by 'Josser' Watling for his sharp dressing as a youngster, was content with his local lot.

Ironically, the boy who became a Rovers hero almost started out with City. Hailing from the Robins' heartland of Knowle West, he was lined up for Ashton Gate. When he arrived to sign he was kept waiting, grew fed up, took a bus to Eastville and put his name on a dotted line for the Pirates instead. Alfie went on to forge lethal alliances, first with Geoff Bradford and then Ian Hamilton, excelling at both centre- and inside-forward and netting a club record of 37 senior goals in 1963/64.

His most high-profile glory came with two strikes in the 1956 FA Cup thrashing of the pre-Munich Busby Babes, 4-0 on an Eastville mud-heap, but this writer cherishes a minor masterpiece in a more prosaic encounter, at home to Bournemouth in October 1964. Alfie beat three men on half-way, strolled away from the stranded defenders and coolly struck a low drive past the 'keeper. That was vintage Biggs.

With a different outlook, he might have won more tangible rewards for all that talent. But, if it's any consolation, no other character from either Eastville or Ashton Gate is remembered with more genuine warmth.

BORN: Bristol, 8.2.36

ROVERS RECORD:

League: 424 games, 178 goals

FA Cup: 26 games, 13 goals

League Cup: 13 games, 6 goals

Total: 463 games, 197 goals

OTHER CLUBS:

Preston North End 61/2-62/3 (49, 22)

Walsall 67/8-68/9 (24, 9)

Swansea Town 68/9 (16, 4)

BORN: Bristol. 18.7.27

DIED: Bristol, 30.12.94

ROVERS RECORD:

League: 461 games, 242 goals

FA Cup: 38 games, 15 goals

League Cup: 12 games, 3 goals

Total: 511 games, 260 goals

ROVERS HONOURS:

Third Division South Championship 52/3

1 England cap 1955

GEOFF BRADFORD

1949/50 — 1963/64

HOPE SPRINGS ETERNAL in the hearts of football supporters, and it is just possible that Bristol Rovers might unearth a player so outstanding that his deeds will eclipse those of every hero who went before him at Eastville, Twerton Park or The Memorial Stadium. But failing the discovery of such a paragon, the popular choice as the greatest performer in the club's 85-year League history to date will remain Geoff Bradford.

Certainly when Geoff was in his goal-scoring prime, the spearhead of the Pirates' exhilarating sides of the 1950s, he was accorded almost Superman status in Bristol. Throughout the rest of the country, meanwhile, often he was the only Rovers player the fans knew.

By modern standards his record is phenomenal, but it is not only that he found the net better than once every two games for 15 years that prompts ex-colleagues and opponents alike to speak of him with a respect bordering on reverence. That reputation also owes much to a staggering technical talent that enabled him to do his job with ruthless efficiency.

Geoff was as clean, accurate and powerful a striker of the ball as could be found anywhere outside the game's very top echelons. Without hesitation he could hit the target with either foot from almost any angle, his ball control was as assured as it was adhesive, and he boasted an intuitive knack of winning aerial duels, invariably appearing to be on the way up when the opposing defender was coming down.

To all these gifts was added a natural resilience that saw him return in triumph from serious leg injuries, sustained at Plymouth in 1953 and Doncaster in 1956, that might have put him out of football for good. His critics called him lazy but Geoff, a retiring individual known as Rip (Van Winkle) to team-mates through his habit of dropping off to sleep before a match, could justifiably refer them to his goal tally.

Glorious milestones abounded throughout the Bradford career. At the time of writing, he remains the only Rovers man to play for England – on his international debut he scored against Denmark, as all at Eastville had expected, but he was never given another chance on the world stage.

Then there was the hat-trick against Newport that clinched promotion from the Third Division in 1953, three strikes at Fulham in the Pirates' first game in the higher grade and, more memorable still, yet another hat-trick, against Stoke at Eastville in April 1954, to mark his comeback from the Plymouth mishap.

That day he played with his knee swathed in yards of bandages, and grown men wept with emotion to see him overcome such adversity. It is conceivable that some Rovers star of the future will emulate, or even surpass, the achievements of Geoff Bradford. But don't hold your breath . . .

MARCUS BROWNING

1989/90 — 1996/97

WHEN MALCOLM ALLISON took over as Rovers manager in 1992, he announced that he had in his squad a player who reminded him of the great Manchester City and England midfielder Colin Bell. Allison went on to predict that Marcus Browning would one day play for England. He claimed, too, that Marcus was the only player in the Rovers squad who walked properly.

Big Mal was correct in his prediction that Browning would play international football, but it was for Wales not England that he earned his five caps while at Rovers, making him one of the few Bristolians to earn full international honours.

Marcus was discovered, while playing as a schoolboy for Whitchurch Sports, by Rovers' youth development manager Roy Dolling, who was in the habit of bringing the pick of young local talent to the club, often plucking the most promising lads from under the noses of Bristol City.

Browning began his career as a centre-forward but switched to midfield and it was in this role that the young fitness fanatic made his impact at Rovers, riveting the attention as a box-to-box runner with a keen eye for goal and a blockbuster shot.

However, it was a loan move to Hereford in 1992 that seemed to spark the boy's potential. He scored five goals in seven games for United and was the subject of a £40,000 bid from Edgar Street. Rovers turned down the offer and Marcus went on to become a key player in John Ward's Rovers squad that peaked with the Wembley play-off final of 1995.

It was a former Rovers boss who spotted Browning's rapid progress and called him into the Wales squad. Bobby Gould discovered that the Hartcliffe lad with the strongest of Bristol accents had Welsh grandparents and gave him his full debut for his country against Italy in 1996.

Back at Rovers, the new international continued to build his fitness and was the only player who was able to challenge Ian Holloway's supremacy in cross-country training runs. Although his first touch wasn't always the most deft, he could dominate the centre of midfield and his surging runs at the heart of the opposition defence often created chances for Hartcliffe namesake Marcus Stewart or Wales team-mate Gareth Taylor. Browning, too, could strike venomously, although one of his most memorable goals for Rovers was a bizarre affair. With the score at 1-1, Brentford goalkeeper Kevin Dearden mistakenly thought he'd heard a whistle and placed the ball for a free-kick. Marcus kicked the ball into an empty net, the goal stood and Rovers won 2-1.

When Huddersfield bought Browning for £450,000 in February 1997, it seemed that he would continue to develop his undoubted potential. But he never settled with the Yorkshire club, soon moving on to Gillingham for £200,000, then being freed to join Bournemouth in 2002. In the long run, Marcus Browning didn't fully realise his vast potential, but at least Rovers fans saw him at his very best.

BORN: Bristol, 22.4.71

ROVERS RECORD:

League: 152 (22) games, 13 goals

FA Cup: 8 games, 1 goal

League Cup: 7 (3) games, 0 goals

Others: 13 (5) games, 3 goals

Total: 180 (30) games, 17 goals

OTHER CLUBS:

Hereford United on loan 92/3 (7, 5)

Huddersfield Town 96/7-98/9 (33, 0)

Gillingham 98/9-01/02 (78, 3)

Bournemouth 02/03- (125, 1)

5 Wales caps 1996-97

BORN: Bristol, 28.8.75

ROVERS RECORD:

League: 165 (9) games, 72 goals

FA Cup: 10 games, 2 goals

League Cup: 7 (1) games, 2 goals

Others: 6 games, 3 goals

Total: 188 (10) games, 79 goals

OTHER CLUBS:

Norwich City 94/5-95/6 (29, 6)

Bournemouth on loan 95/6 (5, 0)

Reading 00/01-02/03 (108, 50)

Busan Icons, South Korea, 03

Queen's Park Rangers 03/04-04/05 (43, 6)

Swindon Town 05/06-

JAMIE CURETON

1996/97 — 2000/01

WHEN THE TERRACE PUNDITS made their way down the Gloucester Road after a hard-fought home win towards the end of the 1990s their thoughts would turn inevitably to the role of Jamie Cureton. 'All he does is score goals' they'd say, before slipping into the Victoria for refreshment or visiting the Bristol Fryer for a fish supper. That was a harsh (and in this case unjustified) criticism of the striker and yet there was an element of truth in it.

Sometimes Cureton drifted out of games and often his strikes came in clusters. Also, he had the unusual habit of scoring many of his goals away from home, so if you happened to catch Jamie in the middle of a barren spell at The Mem, you'd be forgiven for wondering why the slightly built Bristolian was so highly regarded. In fact, his two-season partnership with Jason Roberts which yielded a combined total of 93 goals reveals exactly how important Jamie Cureton was. Although Roberts may be remembered by many admirers as the more prolific scorer, the statistics show that Cureton netted a total of 48 times in 1998/99 and 1999/00, compared with Roberts' tally of 45 hits.

Jason showed all the rough edges which might be expected of a non-League player when he first arrived at Rovers, whereas Cureton was always blessed with more technical ability. Both were excellent finishers although their partnership was not the classic combination of target man and opportunist. Roberts wasn't a great header of the ball while Cureton rarely picked up chances from a route-one clearance, instead proving most effective when a pass was played swiftly to his feet. He was a fine striker of the ball and hit more than his share of goals from the edge of the area.

Cureton was first spotted by Southampton when he was playing in a Bristol schoolboy league, and went to The Dell as a trainee. Eventually he signed as a professional for Norwich, but never established himself in the first team and was delighted to return to his home town when he received the call from Ian Holloway. He scored twice on his home debut against Chesterfield and went on to net four times in his month-long loan spell. It was more than enough to persuade Rovers to pay the £200,000 fee being asked by Norwich.

Admittedly Cureton scored only twice in his next 12 starts but he finished the season with 11 goals, only one fewer than his front-line partner Peter Beadle. The following term Barry Hayles took the plaudits, but in 1998/99 Cureton was Rovers' top scorer, an ever-present menace with 25 goals in 46 games. Remarkably that tally included four second-half strikes away at Reading in a 6-0 victory (the game was scoreless at half time); a hat-trick away at Walsall; two goals at Stoke, another brace at Blackpool and yet another hat-trick at Macclesfield. In 1999/2000 Cureton contributed 22 goals, including a three-goal display at Oxford.

Although many Rovers fans were resigned to losing both Roberts and Cureton at the end of that season, there was much surprise that Jason commanded a fee of £2 million while Jamie departed for a mere £250,000. The reason for the prolific Bristolian's cut-price exit remains a public mystery.

JOE DAVIS

1960/61 — 1966/67

STRAIGHT-TALKING JOE DAVIS was one of Bristol Rovers' most influential post-war captains and capable centre-halves; but, at least in public, he never got the credit he deserved. Ask any former team-mate about Joe and he will recall a man of integrity who demanded total commitment, abhorring cheats above all else, and commanded widespread respect. Though undemonstrative, he could be a persuasive spokesman for his players, and was an unfailing source of soccer wisdom for the club's youngsters.

As a footballer he was undoubtedly underrated, a thinker and organiser who in the mid-1960s meant as much to the Rovers rearguard as Alfie Biggs did to the forward line. Joe, a cousin of Bobby Jones, was competitive in the air despite being unfashionably small for a centre-half, but his prime assets were speed and a sure touch with either foot, unusually constructive attributes for a Third Division defender. Naturally right-sided, he worked assiduously on his left foot at the insistence of his father, an accomplished local player, and it paid off to such a degree that eventually he used it to take penalties with unerring success.

Although his prime was well before the heyday of the sweeper, essentially that was the role Joe took, mopping up behind wing-halves Terry Oldfield and Ray Mabbutt and making full use of his pace and sharpness in the tackle to cover full-backs Doug Hillard and Gwyn Jones.

One of his most outstanding displays was in the infamous encounter at Bradford in April 1963, after which two of his colleagues admitted to taking bribes. Joe performed heroics that day and was largely instrumental in Rovers gaining a point, sorely needed in the battle to avoid relegation. A more cherished memory is of his polished showing against Bobby Charlton, albeit in defeat, at Old Trafford in a 1964 FA Cup clash.

Joe spent his final Eastville campaign at full-back when it was decided that central defence needed the height of young Stuart Taylor, then he moved to Swansea Town, where his career was curtailed by Achilles problems. Later he went on to renew his Pirates link as a scout and youth coach, playing a major part in the development of Paul Randall, Steve White, Gary Penrice and Ian Holloway, among others.

Once again, Joe Davis, whose day job was as field sales manager in the circulation department of the *Bristol Evening Post*, was unobtrusively giving his considerable all for Bristol Rovers.

BORN: Bristol, 24.8.38

ROVERS RECORD:

League: 210 (1) games, 4 goals

FA Cup: 14 games, 2 goals

League Cup: 7 games, 0 goals

Total: 231 (1) games, 6 goals

OTHER CLUBS:

Swansea Town 66/7-67/8 (38, 0)

COLIN DOBSON

1972/73 — 1975/76

COLIN DOBSON was the little left-wing general who brought a touch of top-flight class to Eastville just when it was most needed. For several seasons Rovers had lingered frustratingly on the fringe of the Third Division promotion race, always winning more matches than they lost but forever failing to convince that they had the quality to make that last, decisive stride.

The most obvious difference in the successful campaign of 1973/74 was the pairing of Alan Warboys and Bruce Bannister, but even 'Smash and Grab' needed someone to serve them with ammunition. One productive source was Kenny Stephens on the right flank, but arguably the most telling ingredient in manager Don Megson's lethal mix was Colin's teasing contribution from the left.

The flame-haired north-easterner had learned his trade in the First Division with Sheffield Wednesday, and as he had been one of the most enterprising wingers in the country for five years, his artistry hardly came as a surprise.

At 33 he had lost the speed to go past players, but he was a thinker whose head would always save his legs. With consummate economy of movement he would jink this way and that, wrong-footing his full-back before unveiling the speciality which created so many goals.

Dobson's trump card was his knack of bending accurate, left-foot crosses around defenders and into the path of oncoming forwards. It was an exquisite skill, perfectly tailored for Rovers' two deadly spearheads, and one that opposing teams found huge difficulty in countering. Usually the best they could come up with was double-marking the inventive flankman, which merely created extra space for his team-mates.

Sadly Colin, whose finest hour was as Brighton's tormentor-in-chief at the Goldstone in December 1973, when he inspired an 8-2 victory, was plagued with a painful foot condition that cost him scores of appearances. That was a body blow to the side and it was no coincidence that his only extended first-team run was in the season when Second Division status was finally earned. After that, the genial Dobson was forced to concentrate mainly on coaching, a role in which he excelled for Rovers, and eventually for other clubs in England and abroad.

His stay in Bristol was a credit to all concerned. Megson, a former Sheffield teammate, had taken him on a free transfer from Huddersfield as one of his first managerial acts – and certainly one of his canniest.

BORN: Middlesbrough, Yorkshire, 9.5.40

ROVERS RECORD:

League: 62 games, 4 goals

FA Cup: 3 games, 1 goal

League Cup: 1 game, 0 goals

Others: 2 games, 0 goals

Total: 68 games, 5 goals

ROVERS HONOURS:

Promotion from Third Division 73/4

OTHER CLUBS:

Sheffield Wednesday 61/2-65/6 (177, 49)

Huddersfield Town 66/7-70/1 (155, 50)

Brighton & Hove Albion on loan 71/2 (4, 0)

JIM EADIE

1972/73 — 1976/77

THOSE WHO LAMENT the dearth of characters in modern football will always relish memories of the Flying Pig from Kirkintilloch. He was otherwise known as genial Jim Eadie, and he happened to be one of the most naturally gifted goalkeepers ever to come out of Scotland.

Jim's affectionate nickname – borrowed from former Liverpool custodian Tommy Lawrence – referred with equal candour to his agility and his bulk, and the fans feted him as a swashbuckler who seemed actively to enjoy being placed under heavy pressure. There were games when he appeared to defy marauding opponents almost single-handedly, all the while exuding a beat-me-if-you-can bravado which rendered him irresistible to the Eastville faithful.

Off the pitch he lived life to the full, and was not one who delighted in training. His inevitable summer weight-gain drove manager Don Megson close to despair, culminating in a system by which Jim was fined for each pound he put on during the recess. The 6ft 2in 'keeper accepted the imposition with good humour, turning up for one pre-season photo-call with a giant cream cake with which to taunt his tormentor.

But whatever damage Jim might do to the Eastville scales, there was never any doubt about his talent. When he joined Rovers from Cardiff in early 1973 as a replacement for the injured Dick Sheppard, his prowess was immediately obvious. Eadie used his huge frame and safe hands to dominate the box, routinely pulled off astonishing reflex saves, and could kick the ball the length of the field. He kept clean sheets in his first five games and in the next season was an underrated factor in Rovers' promotion success, once going nearly 700 minutes without conceding a goal.

But the easy-going Scot reserved what was perhaps his finest save for a freezing night at Hereford. Near the end of a game which the 'keeper had spent in icy near-isolation, Dixie McNeil's far-post header looked certain to steal the points. The Eadie response was a plunging scoop reminiscent of Gordon Banks's famous effort against Pele, and later he quipped that he'd imagined he'd been diving for his wage packet!

Jim, a one-time Glasgow Rangers junior, had so much ability that with more ambition he would surely have played for Scotland. Instead he ended up as a free transfer to Bath City in 1977; and long after that he was still soaring through the air in local testimonial games, if not with the greatest of ease exactly, then certainly with a dash of that old buccaneering style. Jim Eadie was always one of a kind.

BORN: Kirkintilloch, Dunbartonshire, 4.2.47

ROVERS RECORD:

League: 183 games, 0 goals

FA Cup: 10 games, 0 goals

League Cup: 11 games, 0 goals

Others: 2 games, 0 goals

Total: 206 games, 0 goals

ROVERS HONOURS:

Promotion from Third Division 73/4

OTHER CLUBS:

Dumbarton

Cardiff City 69/70-70/1 (43, 0)

Chester on loan 72/3 (6, 0)

BORN: Bradford, Yorkshire, 2.7.81

ROVERS RECORD:

League: 76 (40) games, 35 goals

FA Cup: 6 (1) games, 4 goals

League Cup: 7 games, 2 goals

Others: 6 (1) games, 3 goals

Total: 95 (42) games, 44 goals

OTHER CLUBS:

Wigan Athletic 01/02- (134, 59)

NATHAN ELLINGTON

SHYNESS ISN'T A QUALITY immediately associated with centre-forwards, but when Nathan Ellington first arrived at the Rovers training ground, he seemed bashful in the extreme. Maybe Nathan's manner was exaggerated by the extrovert nature of Jason Roberts, who took the youngster under his wing, but such was his modesty that it was natural to wonder if 'The Duke' was in possession of that mean streak so essential to a top-class striker. Appearances proved deceptive, however, as the Yorkshireman revealed himself to be a cruel destroyer of opposition defences.

Rovers were blessed with outstanding strikers in the 1990s – Stewart, Cureton, Roberts and Hayles are the obvious ones, but throughout the decade there was strength in depth through Paul Miller, Gareth Taylor, Peter Beadle, Gui Ipoua and finally the two promising youngsters growing up in the shadow of Cureton and Roberts, Bobby Zamora and Nathan Ellington.

Fans were stunned when Zamora was sold along with Cureton and Roberts at the end of the 1999/00 season, leaving Ellington bereft of a front-line partner, and ultimately Rovers paid the price when they were relegated to the bottom division. But none of this should reflect on the emergence of the graceful, powerful, prolific Nathan Ellington.

He was working as a trainee accountant when Gary Penrice spotted him playing for Walton and Hersham, and despite coming from a non-League background the youngster impressed immediately with his technical ability and all-round athleticism. It came as no surprise to discover that he had set a high jump record for Surrey Schools when he was 15, such was his power in the air.

Ellington illuminated the grim, basement days of the 2001/02 season with League hat-tricks against Leyton Orient and Swansea City to finish the season as top scorer with 15. But his most dazzling display came in the Third Round of the FA Cup when he plundered all the goals in a 3-1 away defeat of Premiership Derby County. It was the first time a Premier League club had been knocked out of the competition by a Third Division team.

This victory was one of Rovers' best in the FA Cup and Nathan was the first Pirate to contribute a hat-trick away from home in the professional game's oldest competition since the club had first entered it in 1895. The feat is worth recording in detail: the first goal was a header over 'keeper Mart Poom; the second followed a solo slalom through the Derby defence, and the third was a right-foot volley.

A national newspaper proclaimed: 'The FA Cup maintained its delightful ability to deliver the unexpected and, in Nathan Ellington, a hero. The young striker's hat-trick ensured that Third Division Rovers not so much bridged the gap between them and their Premiership opponents as rendered it non-existent.'

The spotlight remained on Nathan Ellington as he scored five goals in his next four games and left for Wigan Athletic for £1.2 million on transfer deadline day in March 2002. Later he was reunited with Jason Roberts at the JJB, where they became a formidable goal-scoring duo helping to lift the Latics into the Premiership in 2005. If only such a partnership had been allowed to thrive in Bristol . . .

GEOFF FOX

1947/48 — 1954/55

ASK MOST AGEING FOOTBALL FANS what 1953 means to them and they will recall, instantly and probably with a touch of misty-eyed reverence, the now legendary Matthews Final in which Stan ultimately got his just deserts in the form of an FA Cup winner's medal. Perhaps more masochistic supporters will even hark back to the national team's humiliation at the hands of Hungary, but those who chose to spend their Saturday afternoons at Eastville will lovingly trot out memories of the men who brought unprecedented glory to Bristol Rovers by lifting the Third Division South Championship.

Probe further to ask about that vintage side's defensive qualities and there will be tales of Bamford and Hoyle, Warren and Pitt. It will take a while before they mention left-back Geoff Fox but, when they do, when they conjure up an impression of the man who missed only eight League games in six seasons during the late 1940s and early 1950s, they will talk with respect of a player who did his job and did it well.

Geoff, an all-round sportsman who played cricket for Gloucestershire Seconds, was a young half-back with Bristol City Colts and reached the fringe of the first team before signing for Ipswich Town. Rovers brought him home in June 1947 and soon, under the influence of manager Bert Tann, he was converted into a fast, determined and strong full-back with a penchant for long left-foot passes to his winger 'Josser' Watling. Ironically, it was 'Josser' who was destined eventually to take over Geoff's defensive role, but not before the supremely fit Fox had distinguished himself in a 300-game Rovers career.

An inveterate shouter and organiser on the pitch, Geoff offered a marked contrast to his illustrious partner, the quiet Harry Bamford. Between them they were an effective combination, arguably the finest full-back pairing the club has ever had. One of Geoff's best-remembered performances was in the goalless FA Cup quarter-final at Newcastle in February 1951, and he deserved better fortune than to deflect a drive from Ernie Taylor into his own net during the 3-1 replay defeat.

Ever his own man and extremely self-confident, Geoff enterprisingly planned for the time when he would have to leave football, only to find himself in dispute with the club over his wish to go part-time. Accordingly, in 1955, he moved to Swindon Town before going into business. None who knew him was surprised by his subsequent success.

BORN: Bristol, 19.1.25

DIED: Worcester, 1.1.94

ROVERS RECORD:

League: 276 games, 2 goals

FA Cup: 24 games, 0 goals

Total: 300 games, 2 goals

ROVERS HONOURS:

Third Division South Championship 52/3

OTHER CLUBS:

Ipswich Town 46/7 (11, 1)

Swindon Town 55/6-56/7 (48, 0)

BRIAN GODFREY

1971/72 — 1972/73

KNOWHOW, TRICKS OF THE TRADE, the soccer equivalent of street wisdom, call it what you will; that's what Brian Godfrey brought to Bristol Rovers when he arrived in the summer of 1971 as part of the deal which took Ray Graydon to Aston Villa. Brian was a Welsh international and, although he had played only one First Division match, a decade earlier, he had wide experience of a higher class of football than most of Rovers' essentially youthful squad had sampled. More importantly, he was just the man to pass it on.

Immediately manager Bill Dodgin appointed the much-travelled 31-year-old as skipper; Brian, arguably the Pirates' finest attacking wing-half since Jackie Pitt, responded enthusiastically. An ebullient, sometimes abrasive character who gave the impression that he was in control of every situation, he led by personal example. He believed in a positive approach and demonstrated by his early performances that he could practise what he preached.

The highlight was a hat trick – including two thunderous 25-yarders – in a 7-1 caning of Bradford City at Eastville, though most of that autumn's matches showcased his ball skills, quick thinking and utter determination not to be beaten, attributes which more than compensated for a lack of pace.

The fans warmed to the uncompromising veteran, whose influence was proving especially valuable to fellow midfielder Wayne Jones, and there was much talk of promotion. That didn't materialise, but a Godfrey-driven Rovers side provided League Cup compensation with a run to the quarter-final, falling gloriously to Stoke City in front of 33,000 at Eastville.

The following campaign saw Dodgin's men again finish near the top of the table, but after disagreement over tactics between Brian and his boss the Welshman was sold to Newport for £10,000 in June 1973. Three seasons later he embarked on his own management career, his ports of call including Bath City, Exeter City, Weymouth and Gloucester City, and it surprised many observers that he did not remain in the profession at League level.

Brian spent only two years with Rovers, but that was long enough to make an indelible impression as an inspiring leader and a persuasive spokesman for his players. He is the only man known to have won an argument with Bert Tann, by then general manager and a virtually omnipotent figure at Eastville. Somehow, that says more than anything else about Brian Godfrey.

BORN: Flint, North Wales, 1.5.40

ROVERS RECORD:

League: 79 (2) games, 16 goals

FA Cup: 3 games, 2 goals

League Cup: 12 games, 4 goals

Others: 3 games, 0 goals

Total: 97 (2) games, 22 goals

ROVERS HONOURS:

Watney Cup 72/3

OTHER CLUBS:

Everton 59/60 (1, 0)

Scunthorpe United 60/1-63/4 (87, 24)

Preston North End 63/4-67/8 (122, 52)

Aston Villa 67/8-70/1 (143, 22)

Newport County 73/4-75/6 (118, 14)

Portland Timbers, USA, 75

3 Wales caps (won with Preston North End) 1964-65

MANAGER:

Exeter City 1979-83

BORN: Bristol, 21.7.47

ROVERS RECORD:

League: 131 (2) games, 33 goals

FA Cup: 12 games, 4 goals

League Cup: 10 games, 1 goal

Total: 153 (2) games, 38 goals

OTHER CLUBS:

Aston Villa 71/2-76/7 (193, 67)

Coventry City 77/8 (20, 5)

Washington Diplomats, USA

Oxford United 78/9-80/1 (42, 10)

MANAGER:

Walsall 1998-2002, Bristol Rovers 2002-04

RAY GRAYDON

1965/66 — 1970/71

RAY GRAYDON was the headstrong runaway who left Eastville to prove his mettle. The dashing, blond winger for whom Harold Jarman was shifted from right to left flank in the late 1960s could run like the wind, and many a Third Division full-back felt his draught. But there were times, too many for comfort, when he seemed to be wearing blinkers.

As a youngster Ray impressed Rovers' coaches with his speed, strength and confidence, and was taken on as an apprentice. But the management had doubts, and he was advised to find a trade outside the game. Ironically, it was during his subsequent spell as a part-timer, when training as an electrician, that his full potential became apparent.

Ray was given his League debut at Swansea in September 1965, and for three seasons he made intermittent appearances in the side. His progress was fitful. On many occasions he looked an exciting prospect, slicing through defences and crossing the ball on the run; on others he was dismal, not releasing the ball at the right time and running into blind alleys without a hint of tactical awareness.

To his eternal credit, however, he never knew when he was beaten and, if an opponent dumped him on the seat of his pants a dozen times, Ray would get up and try again. Often he would break through at the umpteenth attempt, a tribute to sheer resilience.

Towards the end of the decade Ray was making more of his talent, and was rewarded with a regular place. By then he had learned to cut inside his full-back, and, although his finishing tended to be wayward, his scorching shot produced some spectacular goals. In 1969/70 there was a spell of nine in 14 games and the big clubs began to take an interest, but it was early in the following campaign, when he scored and excelled in a 1-1 draw at Villa Park, that he paved the way for his exit from Eastville.

In June 1971 he signed for Villa in exchange for Brian Godfrey and £25,000, and it proved the perfect move for him. With the Midlanders he matured into an accomplished player, helping them rise from Third to First Division and win the League Cup twice, scoring the Wembley winner against Norwich in 1975.

Further travels preceded the assistant managership of Oxford United, then came a coaching job at Southampton and a creditable stint in charge of Walsall. In 2002 the affable Bristolian appeared to be the ideal candidate to take over at The Memorial Stadium, being widely experienced and endowed with a deep feeling for the club, but his spell at Rovers' helm was a troubled one, and he left a disappointed man.

BORN: Bath, Somerset, 8.7.42

ROVERS RECORD:

League: 163 games, 0 goals

FA Cup: 10 games, 0 goals

League Cup: 9 games, 0 goals

Total: 182 games, 0 goals

BERNARD HALL

1961/62 — 1966/67

THE COURAGE BERNARD HALL took with him every time he walked on to a football field was destined to cost him his career – and very nearly his life.

There was never any question of the diminutive goalkeeper ducking out of the challenge when Johnny Williams's back-pass stuck in the penalty area mire on a dull New Year's Eve afternoon at Eastville in 1966. Bernard and Middlesbrough's John O'Rourke collided sickeningly. The combative centre-forward hobbled away, ruefully rubbing his thigh; Bernard, all too ominously, lay motionless in the mud.

For days he remained unconscious in hospital, hovering between life and death. Gradually, with football fans all over the country willing him on, he recovered, but his heart-rending attempts to regain full fitness were doomed to failure. Though he was able to live a normal life outside the game, it was a cruel end to a Rovers career that had begun, by chilling coincidence, with the 16-year-old rookie being knocked unconscious on his debut for the reserves.

Typically undeterred, Bernard worked to make the grade, and was given his first-team chance standing in for the injured Howard Radford at home to Charlton in April 1962.

He made a quartet of fine saves and was clearly an exciting prospect, despite some fears that, at 5ft 10in, he would always struggle to deal with crosses.

When the next break came, as a deputy for new signing Esmond Million, he had a disappointing game and was resigned to go back to learning his trade in the stiffs. But then Million was suspended in the 1963 bribes scandal, and this time Bernard cemented his place with some splendid performances, displaying sharp reflexes, a safe pair of hands and a prophetically unnerving willingness to dive among the boots.

A highlight of his first full term as a senior was a starring role at Old Trafford in a 4-1 FA Cup defeat in January 1964. Denis Law scored a hat-trick that day; but as the impish Scot said after the match, had it not been for Bernard he might have scored six.

Apart from one temporary loss of form in late 1965, the popular and easy-going Bathonian – whose idea of time-keeping did not always endear him to his meticulous boss Bert Tann – kept up a consistently high standard. A long-term Rovers future seemed a certainty; then came that fateful New Year's Eve, and soccer oblivion at the age of 24.

IAN HAMILTON

1958/59 — 1967/68

IAN HAMILTON was the stealthiest of strikers. At his best he would ghost through defences like a thief in the night, often anticipating a careless back-pass and having the ability to capitalise on the error; on an off day he could be a frustrating performer, profligate with chances and irritating to fans who saw him, wrongly, as lazy.

Ian was, in fact, an industrious and talented inside-forward whose naturally loose running style belied a willingness to forage and battle which often went unnoticed. Those who played against him speak of an awkward customer who could never be underestimated, especially in the box; team-mates jokingly dubbed him 'Sir Laurence' for winning penalties by his acting!

He specialised in unorthodox, darting runs which unsettled defenders accustomed to a more direct approach, and, though he wasn't the paciest of straight-line sprinters, his speed on the turn often produced a shot from an unexpected angle.

The son of pre-war Rovers wing-half John Hamilton, Ian made his debut in 1958, but with men like Geoff Bradford, Alfie Biggs and Dai Ward on the scene he couldn't claim a regular place for four years. On his breakthrough he forged a fruitful liaison with Alfie, helping 'The Baron' to break the club's scoring record in 1963/64, then he topped the chart himself with 22 goals the following term, despite missing 13 games with the knee trouble that would eventually end his career.

Ian fed hungrily off the big man's service, and it's fair to say that he was to Alf what Bannister was to Warboys a decade later, though arguably he offered rather more of a reciprocal arrangement than did his 1970s counterpart.

One of Hamilton's most significant contributions in ten years as a Pirate came in May 1963 at Halifax, where his match-winning brace of headers, one powerful and the other delicately steered, staved off relegation to the Fourth Division. But it was a less productive feat at Southend in September 1964 that won him a place in the archives. That day he found the net three times in a 6-3 defeat, thus becoming the first Rovers man to score a hat trick and finish on the losing side.

When cartilage problems struck he was 24 and apparently approaching his peak. Though he made a few appearances in subsequent seasons he was never again the incisive force who had promised so much. His playing days limped to a sad end at Newport and Ian, who went on to work for Rolls-Royce in Bristol, was left to reflect on soccer's fickle fates.

BORN: Bristol, 12.9.40

ROVERS RECORD:

League: 149 games, 60 goals

FA Cup: 11 games, 1 goal

League Cup: 9 games, 6 goals

Total: 169 games, 67 goals

OTHER CLUBS:

Exeter City on loan 67/8 (4, 1)

Newport County 68/9 (15, 2)

BORN: Lambeth, London, 17.5.72

ROVERS RECORD:

League: 62 games, 32 goals

FA Cup: 5 games, 2 goals

League Cup: 4 games, 1 goal

Others: 3 (2) games, 1 goal

Total: 74 (2) games, 36 goals

OTHER CLUBS:

Fulham 98/9-03/04 (175, 44)

Sheffield United 04/05 (4, 0)

Millwall 04/05- (32, 12)

Jamaica caps.

BARRY HAYLES

WHEN IAN HOLLOWAY was scouting Barry Hayles in the Vauxhall Conference, he watched the powerful Stevenage Borough striker in action against Woking Town, and saw him marked out of the game by centre-half Steve Foster. As a result Rovers signed the imposing stopper in May 1997, and, a couple of months later, forked out £200,000 to ensure that the two former non-League rivals lined up together as the Pirates kicked off the next term.

Hayles responded majestically, equalling the achievements of Vic Lambden in 1946/47 and Dennis Bailey in 1988/89 of finding the net in his first three League outings for the club, then proved it was no fluke by finishing his first season in League football as the Second Division's highest scorer with 23 goals.

Barry was a quietly spoken, modest character off the field but once he pulled on the Rovers shirt he was transformed into a fearsome powerhouse and a scourge of defences. He was blessed with a rare instinct for reading the game and frequently he could find that extra yard of space that separates a great striker from a good one. Indeed, many Rovers fans would name the muscular Londoner as one of the club's finest ever forwards. Like two other classy marksmen who flourished in the blue-and-white quarters, Marcus Stewart and Jason Roberts, Hayles played in the Premier League, and of the three, arguably, he looked the most accomplished at the highest level.

To employ modern coaching terminology, Barry benefited from exceptional 'peripheral vision', though an older generation would be more comfortable in talking of the striker's instinct or his knack for being in the right place at the right time. Whatever, it was his ability to analyse exactly what was going on around him and anticipate other players' movement that enabled him to unlock the tightest of rearguards. Crucially, too, he could finish clinically, and once he'd created his opening, it seemed to Rovers fans that a goal was inevitable.

Hayles wasn't a selfish player, but he tended to carve out his own chances rather than act as provider for partners. He was a decent crosser and adept at gliding or powering his way towards goal from either flank, but Barry preferred to play his football in a central role. He was at his most effective around the edge of the penalty area and it was in this territory that he terrorised the Second Division. His explosive pace and his capacity to deploy brute force or exquisite finesse earned him approximately one goal in every two League outings for Rovers, a fabulous strike-rate in today's game.

It's difficult to pick out a single Barry Hayles performance for particular praise, but it's fun to reminisce, and who could forget his winner against Brentford in the final game of 1997/98 that took the Pirates into the play-offs? Or his last goal in a Rovers shirt, involving a stunning turn and volley from outside the box against Walsall in October 1998?

You pays your money and takes your choice, but the most telling tribute of all is that there was no such thing as a typical Barry Hayles goal. He scored them anyhow and from anywhere.

BORN: Bristol, 10.8.35

DIED: Bristol, 6.1.97

ROVERS RECORD:

League: 313 (5) games, 12 goals

FA Cup: 24 games, 1 goal

League Cup: 15 games, 0 goals

Total: 352 (5) games, 13 goals

DOUG HILLARD

1958/59 — 1967/68

DOUG HILLARD was a rough diamond of a right-back whose barn-door frame, pugnacious crew-cut and heart that might have been engraved with blue-and-white quarters seemed to defy the world to take on his beloved Bristol Rovers. Classy he was not, but, if there was one man to have on your side when the enemy threatened to cross that final ditch, then this most outstanding of clubmen would have taken a deal of beating.

He was recruited from local football as an inside-forward, a role to which his dash and determination were suited, though his ball skills were not. At Eastville he was quickly converted to a defender and then worked fiendishly to improve all aspects of his game. Doug's application was rewarded when he became the long-term replacement for Harry Bamford after Brian Doyle had filled in during the immediate aftermath of the elegant veteran's fatal accident.

The enthusiastic youngster made the position his own for the next ten years, his speed and power in the tackle making him especially effective against strong, direct wingers such as Peter McParland of Aston Villa. Sometimes he came unstuck against tricky flankmen in the mould of Norwich City's Bill Punton, but invariably he enjoyed success against the immensely gifted Don Rogers of Swindon.

As an attacking force, Doug was ideally suited to the Rovers' style. On gaining possession his preferred option was the long ball down the wing or the inside-right channel for Alfie Biggs to nod down to another forward or run on to himself; thus was defence turned into offence with one raking pass.

If Alfie was tightly marked then Doug relished a periodic sortie over the half-way line, opponents seeming to fall away from him as he progressed. But as a rule he remained wisely in his familiar slot, allowing more creative colleagues to take the initiative.

The one occasion when manager Bert Tann threw Hillard into uncharted territory, as an emergency striker at Scunthorpe in September 1961, ended in personal disaster. Doug challenged the 'keeper for a 50-50 ball and a sound like the snapping of a dry stick echoed around the ground. The broken leg sidelined him for seven months, his only prolonged absence from the team.

On retirement, Doug succeeded with a sports equipment business and also went into local soccer management with Taunton Town and Mangotsfield United. Life without football was inconceivable for a man born to be a Pirate.

BORN: Bristol, 12.3.63

ROVERS RECORD:

League: 379 (18) games, 41 goals

FA Cup: 26 games, 4 goals

League Cup: 21 games, 1 goal

Others: 27 games, 3 goals

Total: 453 (18) games, 49 goals

ROVERS HONOURS:

Third Division Championship 89/90

Leyland Daf Cup Finalist 89/90

OTHER CLUBS:

Wimbledon 85/6 (19, 2)

Brentford 85/6-87/8 (30, 2)

Torquay United on loan 86/7 (5, 0)

Queen's Park Rangers 91/2-95/6 (147, 4)

MANAGER:

Bristol Rovers 1996-2001

Queen's Park Rangers 2001-

IAN HOLLOWAY

1980/81 — 1984/85, 1987/88 — 1990/91, 1996/97 — 1998/99

IAN HOLLOWAY performed a noble service for a new generation of Rovers fans. After his passionate appearance on the scene, no longer could old-timers look back to vintage years when men were men and footballers were ready to sweat blood for the Pirates and then shake their heads and proclaim: 'They don't make 'em like that any more.' In fact they did, and Ian Holloway was there to prove it.

No one in the modem era has symbolised the spirit of the Rovers quite as vividly as the 5ft 7in midfield general with the soul of a workaholic fighting cock. Gerry Francis's 1989/90 Third Division Champions were essentially a side without stars, but the biggest single on-the-field influence was unquestionably the lad from Cadbury Heath, who had returned from an unhappy sojourn in the Smoke to win glory with his first footballing love.

Back in the 1970s, such heights of achievement were no more than distant dreams to the tiny but fiercely dedicated schoolboy who put himself through twice-daily weight-training sessions to add much-needed muscle to a frame which, though apparently frail, was deceptively wiry. With the constant support of his father Bill – a much-loved figure in local football who tragically did not live to see his son's finest hours – Ian strove towards his goal of becoming a professional.

Rovers gave him his chance as an industrious winger, and during his first extended senior run in 1982/83 his skill and commitment often limited Mick Channon to a place on the substitutes' bench. Such was his progress that in July 1985 he attracted a £35,000 bid from Wimbledon, then in Division Two and rising fast. Rovers were glad of the cash and off he went, but injury and illness limited his chances, both at Plough Lane and subsequently at Brentford.

It was then that Gerry Francis pulled off what was arguably the finest transfer coup of his career. Knowing the parlous state of his employers' coffers, the manager loaned them the £10,000 needed to take Ian to Twerton Park, and received a rich dividend for his outlay. Eventually moving from the wing to midfield, the Eastville old boy was an inspiration. Every manoeuvre seemed to involve him; he harassed opponents increasingly, was adept at working tight-passing triangles, and as his game developed he became capable of ambitious through-balls. On the run-in to the title Ian played through the pain of a damaged knee, refusing to miss a minute of the action, as near to being indispensable as any individual could be.

Ian went on to prove himself in the top flight with Queen's Park Rangers before making a second return to Bristol Rovers as player-boss in 1996. For three seasons he remained a key member of the side before laying aside his boots and continuing to strive against mounting financial odds as manager until a run of dire results midway through 2000/01 cost him his job. With typical grit, he resurrected his career back at Loftus Road, emerging as one of the League's most colourful characters.

PETER HOOPER

1953/54 — 1961/62

PETER HOOPER was a man with an explosive trademark. In his prime he possessed what was probably the hardest shot in professional football, and shrewd contemporary observers swear they would rather have stood in the path of a 20-yard rocket from Bobby Charlton or Peter Lorimer than a left-foot Hooper humdinger from twice the distance.

When the curly-haired Devonian arrived at Eastville from non-League soccer in 1953, it quickly became apparent that Rovers had acquired a potential match-winner, and it wasn't long before Peter had ousted experienced outside-left 'Josser' Watling. He even posed problems in training because few volunteers could be found to man the defensive wall when he practised free-kicks, and he proceeded to cut a dash in the Second Division.

Naturally, dead-ball situations were a speciality, but there was one occasion when his power backfired. Near the end of a close-fought encounter with Leicester City, the Rovers were awarded a penalty. Peter stepped up for what normally was a formality, but this time he slammed the ball against a post so hard that it rebounded almost to the halfway line. The Bristol defenders were so dumbfounded that they stood and stared, and the Foxes broke away to score the winner.

Though lurid descriptions of his long-range marksmanship dominated his news cuttings, soon it was clear that his left foot was good for more than propelling high-velocity missiles towards hapless goalkeepers. Peter could also cross the ball accurately and often revealed the flair to go past defenders, though there was a tendency to drift out of a game after being hit by a crunching tackle.

As the decade drew to a close, calls mounted for international recognition, and in 1960 he was selected for the Football League. By this time the Pirates were struggling, and when they were relegated two years later the popular winger moved to Cardiff for £10,500.

Despite doing well at Ninian Park he failed to settle and returned to Bristol, this time at Ashton Gate, in July 1963. After overcoming an illness, he performed creditably enough for the old enemy without ever recapturing the golden touch of his early days.

There followed a short Southern League stint at Worcester before he went West once more, first taking a Devon pub and then joining the probation service, secure in the knowledge that he had left an indelible mark on Bristol football. Not to mention a few goalposts and defensive walls . . .

BORN: Teignmouth, Devon, 2.2.33

ROVERS RECORD:

League: 297 games, 101 goals

FA Cup: 18 games, 5 goals

League Cup: 6 games, 1 goal

Total: 321 games, 107 goals

OTHER CLUBS:

Cardiff City 62/3 (40, 22)

Bristol City 63/4-65/6 (54, 14)

BERT HOYLE

1950/51 — 1952/53

BRISTOL ROVERS' TINY WINGER George Petherbridge turned smartly after scoring a memorable goal past Exeter City's towering goalkeeper Bert Hoyle and jogged jauntily towards the half-way line. Suddenly the supporters' cheers were stilled to silence. The beaten custodian was hurtling out of his goal and bearing down on the retreating back of one of the smallest men in League football. There were those in the crowd on that chilly February afternoon in 1949 who feared that the little man had played his last game. There was a gasp from the terraces as Big Bert seized George by the shoulder, spun him round – and shook him warmly by the hand.

The incident typified Bert, a warm, jovial character who joined Rovers 15 months later for £350 and went on to help them claim the Third Division South Championship in 1952/53. He got on famously with the fans, chatting to them in idle moments during matches. They quickly built up a rapport with the extrovert 'keeper and never was this more evident than on the day it rained oranges at Eastville.

The Pirates were in the middle of their momentous 1951 FA Cup run, and before one home tie a newspaper revealed Bert's habit of keeping an orange in his cap at the back of his net for periodic refreshment. As the popular Yorkshireman took his place between the posts, his sizeable fan club showered him with fruit. This continued intermittently throughout the match and once, with Bert strolling around his penalty box gathering stray oranges to stack in the goal, the visitors launched an unexpected assault. Team-mates later reckoned they had never seen their burly last line of defence move so fast.

In fact Bert's apparently light-hearted attitude masked the professional approach of a man who took his game very seriously. Before a match he would compose himself in solitude and then burst into the dressing room exhorting his colleagues to heroic efforts. His style was to command the area, and when he went for the ball whoever was in the way had to move. Sooner or later, most of his defenders picked up a black eye or a thick ear after being flattened by a Hoyle charge.

Bert's days at Eastville were brought to a premature end when he suffered a serious head injury in an accident while driving home to Devon after keeping a clean sheet against Bristol City in February 1953. He'd played enough matches to qualify for a championship medal; but he was never able to return to football, and took a pub in Dawlish Warren.

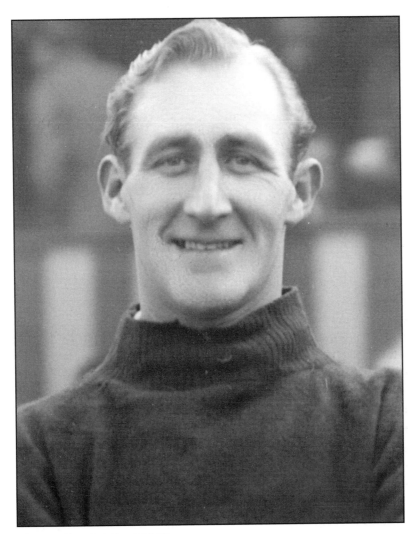

BORN: Baildon, Yorkshire, 22.4.20

DIED: Torbay, 7.03

ROVERS RECORD:

League: 105 games, 0 goals

FA Cup: 19 games, 0 goals

Total: 124 games, 0 goals

ROVERS HONOURS:

Third Division South Championship 52/3

OTHER CLUBS:

Exeter City 46/7-49/50 (82, 0)

BORN: Bristol, 4.5.39

ROVERS RECORD:

League: 440 (12) games, 127 goals

FA Cup: 33 games, 7 goals

League Cup: 29 (1) games, 9 goals

Total: 502 (13) games, 143 goals

OTHER CLUBS:

Newport County 73/4 (40, 8)

New York Cosmos

MANAGER:

Bristol Rovers 1979-80

HAROLD JARMAN

1959/60 — 1972/73

IMAGINE THE DREARIEST of winter afternoons, a chill mist descending like a shroud to trap the all-pervading odour of gas in a dank Eastville. On the pitch the football is as grey as the day; on the terraces a few thousand dispirited souls marvel at the dogged faith that has dragged them from their firesides.

Suddenly the ball arrives at the feet of a forlorn-looking individual, loitering languidly near the half-way line, and the crowd's desultory buzz takes on a new, expectant note. The slim figure shuffles forward slowly, almost tentatively, and then, abruptly transformed, spurts into action.

Dipping one of those drooping shoulders, he swerves round a startled defender, feints past a second and outstrips a third with sheer, destructive pace before unleashing a shot from the angle of the penalty box, a drive of such venom and velocity that it rebounds from the goal stanchion before the diving 'keeper hits the ground. There's a split second of unbelieving silence and then the Eastville roar rends the air. Harold Jarman has struck again.

Such a scene – give or take the odd detail – was not rare in the 1960s, when Bristol's most gifted post-war flankman was in his pomp. Harold did have his critics, though, notably for his work-rate, and in his early days he was barracked by the same denizens of the North

Enclosure who were later to form his personal fan club.

One facet lacking from his make-up was confidence, which helps explain why his talent, unquestionably of First Division standard, was never displayed in the top flight; the Alf Ramsey-inspired obsession with workhorses rather than wingers also worked against him.

Rovers, of course, were happy to keep this self-effacing Bristolian who could play on either flank, and he went on to score more goals for the Pirates than anyone except Geoff Bradford and Alfie Biggs, an astonishing feat for a winger.

Harold, also a Gloucestershire cricketer, ended his League days with Newport County before enjoying an Indian summer with New York Cosmos, who were in no doubt about his value. When he left they replaced him with Pele!

Twice more he was to answer the Eastville call, once as the caretaker boss who saved them from relegation in 1980, only to be replaced by Terry Cooper, and then as a youth coach destined for redundancy. After that he reverted to his trade as a carpenter, but it is for his artistry on the wing that the name of Harold Jarman will be forever revered. He proved that football, for all its problems, can still be a beautiful game.

BORN: Bristol, 28.10.38

ROVERS RECORD:

League: 410 (11) games, 101 goals

FA Cup: 28 games, 5 goals

League Cup: 23 (1) games, 4 goals

Total: 461 (12) games, 110 goals

OTHER CLUBS:

Northampton Town 66/7 (18, 1)

Swindon Town 66/7 (11, 0)

BOBBY JONES

1957/58 — 1966/67 & 1967/68 — 1972/73

NOT FOR NOTHING was Bobby Jones known as 'The Eastville Flier'. A bundle of energy with jets in his boots, arguably he was as quick as anyone in the League during his 1960s prime, often breathing life into the most mediocre of games with one thrilling burst of speed.

Bobby, who played much of his football on the left wing despite his preference for an inside-forward role, would push the ball past his marker and sprint after it, leaving all but the most rapid of defenders trailing in his wake. Terrace wags would have it that, if the gate in the Stapleton Road corner of the ground was left open, Bob wouldn't stop running until he reached the city centre.

It was an affectionate joke that nevertheless offered a clue as to why his phenomenal pace didn't take him all the way to the highest class. At times he was simply too fast, plunging headlong into trouble when a more composed approach might have paid dividends; certainly there was a case for a more subtle and varied use of that stunning acceleration.

But it would be churlish to carp over the very strength that made the man who scored more than a century of goals, including two on his debut at Middlesbrough in 1957, one of the best attackers in the Pirates' history.

In fact he had much more to offer than a clean pair of heels, packing a powerful shot in either foot, a greater degree of skill than he was often credited with, and above all, a burning loyalty to Bristol in general and the Rovers in particular.

When a £17,000 transfer to Second Division Northampton became financially imperative in September 1966, Bobby departed rather reluctantly. Predictably for such a confirmed home bird, he didn't settle with the Cobblers, and was delighted to return for £8,000, after the briefest of interludes at Swindon, just 11 months later.

His sparkling form as a deputy for the injured Alfie Biggs in 1964/65 bore out his opinion that he could be more effective in a central position, and later he demonstrated his versatility even further with a capable spell at right-back. Eventually he was released in May 1973, after which, apart from a coaching stint back at Eastville, he became a bastion of local soccer, his chief credit being a six-year spell as boss of Bath City. Bobby Jones remains today what he has always been, a credit to the game he loves and one of the nicest men in football.

VAUGHAN JONES

1976/77 — 1981/82 & 1984/85 — 1992/93

VAUGHAN JONES was living proof that you can't keep a good man down. The versatile Welsh defender was sacked by Bristol Rovers, dumped by Newport County and discarded by Cardiff City – and all by the age of 25. That he bounced back to become a key figure in the Pirates' resurgence and skipper them through the most triumphant campaign in their history speaks volumes for his resilience, self-belief and, not least, his footballing ability.

The most frustrating aspect of Vaughan's early travails was that each time he was rejected he had been playing well. His exit from Eastville when he was freed by Bobby Gould in the summer of 1982 followed his most successful season to date. Playing at right-back, he had missed only a handful of matches and had looked to be one of the young men around whom the manager would build a side capable of ensuring recently relegated Rovers' speedy return to the Second Division.

Sojourns with his two homeland clubs offered no better fortune, and when David Williams brought him back across the Severn Bridge in December 1984, initially on loan as experienced first-team cover, Vaughan might have been forgiven for wondering if yet another disappointment was around the corner. Then, when central defender Aiden McCaffrey was injured, he filled the breach so well that the position became his own. In the next two seasons, with Gould once more in charge, he consolidated; and the arrival of Gerry Francis in July 1987 gave him renewed impetus.

Under Gerry, Vaughan's performances acquired a new edge. He had always been strong in both the air and the tackle, a fair passer of the ball and an acute reader of the game, but now he took on added authority, to the extent that he eventually became a resourceful, vociferous captain who led by example. His adaptability was another useful quality, and it proved invaluable when he switched to left-back to accommodate the emergence of Steve Yates in the centre.

His role in winning the 1989/90 Third Division Championship and reaching the Leyland Daf Cup Final at Wembley, where Tranmere denied him the glory of holding the trophy aloft in his testimonial season, was unobtrusive but crucial. Somehow, amid all the euphoria, those three rejections which had set Vaughan's career back on its heels suddenly seemed a very long time ago.

Still the Welshman had plenty to contribute, proving a trusty bulwark as Rovers consolidated back in the higher grade in 1990/91, but then a broken leg sidelined him for 14 months and he never regained his impetus, making his final appearance as a Pirate in the spring of 1993.

BORN: Tonyrefail, Glamorgan, 2.9.59

ROVERS RECORD:

League: 370 (11) games, 12 goals

FA Cup: 22 games, 1 goal

League Cup: 19 (3) games, 0 goals

Others: 26 games, 0 goals

Total: 437 (14) games, 13 goals

ROVERS HONOURS:

Third Division Championship 89/90

Leyland Daf Cup Finalist 89/90

OTHER CLUBS:

Newport County 82/3-83/4 (68, 4)

Cardiff City 84/5 (11, 0)

BORN: Treorchy, Glamorgan, 20.10.48

ROVERS RECORD:

League: 218 (6) games, 28 goals

FA Cup: 14 (2) games, 3 goals

League Cup: 18 games, 4 goals

Others: 3 games, 0 goals

Total: 253 (8) games, 35 goals

ROVERS HONOURS:

Watney Cup 72/3

1 Wales cap 1971

WAYNE JONES

1966/67 — 1972/73

AS PERSONAL DISASTERS GO, it was an unspectacular affair. There was no one within yards of Wayne Jones when the richly talented Welsh international inside-forward turned with the ball, twisted his knee and fell to the ground in Rovers' Third Division encounter with Brentford at Eastville in November 1972. He was in agony and cartilage trouble was suspected, but when the joint was opened up it was found to be riddled with arthritis. Wayne never played again.

It was a crushing personal blow to the baby-faced play-maker, who at 24 had looked set for an outstanding career. He was the creative hub of a promising side with ambitions of promotion, the subject of intense interest from several of the country's leading clubs – and, perhaps most exciting of all, he had been recalled to the Welsh squad for the forthcoming World Cup qualifier against England.

The loss to Bristol Rovers was incalculable. Wayne, likened by Eastville boss Bill Dodgin to a young Wilf Mannion, either would have fetched a hefty fee on the transfer market or been a significant asset to the Pirates when they eventually reached the Second Division in 1974. With such a classy midfielder, or with replacements bought with the proceeds of his sale, they might have achieved rather more than to endure seven seasons of travail before sinking back to the Third.

Later Wayne served several clubs as a physiotherapist, including Huddersfield Town, and also put in a stint as Rovers' assistant manager under David Williams.

But it is as one of the most polished performers ever to grace Eastville that he will be remembered most vividly. What made him so special? Certainly he was gifted with immaculate ball control, tremendous confidence and a fierce shot, but it was none of those attributes that really marked him out. Wayne's golden gifts were his vision, which enabled him to spot the most unlikely of openings, and his ability to pass the ball over long distances, instantly, accurately and without telegraphing his intentions.

That made him an entertainer of rare quality, and if he had a temperamental side – perhaps being too easily upset by his own mistakes, and prone to drift out of the occasional game – it was because he was a perfectionist, hardly the most damning of character traits.

It's no consolation now to note that in his final season Wayne had at last allied consistency to his customary brilliance. How sad to reflect that we, and he, will never know just how good he might have become.

BORN: Bristol, 24.10.25

DIED: Bristol, 3.7.96

ROVERS RECORD:

League: 269 games, 117 goals

FA Cup: 31 games, 16 goals

Total: 300 games, 133 goals

ROVERS HONOURS:

Third Division South Championship 52/3

VIC LAMBDEN

1945/46 — 1954/55

THE SIGHT OF VIC LAMBDEN surging through the mud like a runaway plough was one of the most fearsome prospects to face Third Division South goalkeepers in the early 1950s. Energetic Vic, one the fastest and strongest centre-forwards of his day, positively thrived in quagmires that bogged down more delicate talents, and it was on heavy grounds that he emerged most often from the shadow of Geoff Bradford, his more illustrious striking partner.

Comparisons with the brilliant Bradford were acutely unfair to Vic who, without possessing extravagant skills, was an accomplished performer in his own right. He was a punishing, hustling marksman with a fierce if periodically wayward shot, and at his peak he netted 84 League and FA Cup goals in three seasons, as well as creating scores of opportunities for Geoff by his selfless running off the ball. As a pair they presented a nightmarish combination for opposing defenders, constantly swapping positions and roaming to either wing.

The industrious Vic was very much a players' player and, though he might have been underrated at times by fans and pundits, and perhaps even lacked confidence in his own ability, there was never any doubt about his value in the minds of team-mates.

They admired his athletic leading of the forward line, always making himself available to either the left-sided long-ball contingent of Fox, Sampson and Watling or the one-two passing combinations of Bamford, Pitt and Petherbridge on the right. His successful linking of two such contrasting styles of approach play was a vital element in both the stirring run to the FA Cup quarter-final in 1951 and triumph in the title race two years later.

During that glorious 1952/53 campaign Vic was rumoured to be a target of several First Division clubs, but in those days manager Bert Tann would have no truck with the transfer market. So the man who could count among his achievements the fastest strike in Rovers' history – an opportunistic effort after eight seconds of an FA Cup-tie with Aldershot in which he went on to score a hat trick – was destined to see out his professional career at Eastville.

Ironically, he was injured early in the next season, and after a lengthy lay-off he was never again the same dynamic force. Deprived of his place first by Barrie Meyer and then by Alfie Biggs, Vic, a cheerful individual who became a postman, moved out of League football to join Trowbridge Town.

LARRY LLOYD

1968/69

BILL SHANKLY was looking for a centre-half. The Liverpool boss needed a long-term replacement for his Scottish colossus, Ron Yeats, and had been pondering the merits of Larry Lloyd, the young but exceedingly green giant who was still in his first season at the heart of Bristol Rovers' defence.

One night in March 1969, Bill crossed the Pennines to Oakwell, where Barnsley were playing host to the West Countrymen, to check the lad's form. Larry had a stinker, continually roaming out of position as the home forwards ran amok and the Tykes won 4-2. Shanks left after an hour and everyone assumed that was the end of the matter, but a few weeks later the 20-year-old was on his way to Anfield in a £50,000 deal which made him, at the time, Bristol's costliest soccer export.

Despite the youngster's poor showing at Barnsley, Shankly had seen the qualities – ruthless aggression, prodigious strength and a burning desire to win – that were to turn Lloyd into a First Division star and England international.

Rovers, in desperate need of cash at the time, were delighted with the transaction; but in playing terms they could ill afford the loss of authority in their back four. Despite a lack of pace and an occasional tendency to lose composure under pressure, Larry, who had established a regular place alongside the less physical but even taller Stuart Taylor after only a year in the reserves, had been crucial in the relegation scrap.

Yet there had been a time when it had seemed unlikely that he would make the grade. The story goes that he was unimpressive in the Eastville youth team and was on the verge of being released when his sister, who was general manager Bert Tann's secretary, mentioned that Bristol City were showing interest in him. Bert decreed that the lad should have another chance and, after Larry had been coached intensively by Bill Dodgin and Bobby Campbell, the decision bore the mark of inspiration.

His eventual move to Merseyside brought medals galore, and after a lean period with Coventry City he went on to European Cup glory with Nottingham Forest. Later Larry ran a pub in Nottingham, but he sampled management, and had hopes of the Eastville hot seat when Bobby Gould left in 1983. It was not to be; David Williams got the job and the towering ex-Rover was denied what would have been a popular return.

BORN: Bristol, 6.10.48

ROVERS RECORD:

League: 43 games, 1 goal

FA Cup: 7 games, 0 goals

League Cup: 1 game, 0 goals

Total: 51 games, 1 goal

OTHER CLUBS:

Liverpool 69/70-73/4 (150, 4)

Coventry City 74/5-76/7 (50, 5)

Nottingham Forest 76/7-80/1 (148, 6)

Wigan Athletic 80/1-82/3 (52, 2)

4 England caps (3 won with Liverpool, 1 with Nottingham Forest) 1971-80

MANAGER:

Wigan Athletic 1981-83

Notts County 1983-84

BORN: Bristol, 23.8.61

ROVERS RECORD:

League: 122 (9) games, 10 goals

FA Cup: 6 (1) games, 1 goal

League Cup: 10 games, 1 goal

Total: 138 (10) games, 12 goals

OTHER CLUBS:

Tottenham Hotspur 82/3-97/8 (477, 27)

16 England caps

(won with Tottenham Hotspur)1982-92

GARY MABBUTT

1978/79 — 1981/82

THE STORY OF GARY MABBUTT stands as an inspiration to any young player not blessed with outstanding natural ability, yet who is determined to make the utmost of what assets he has. That is not to denigrate a superb professional who gave sterling service to Bristol Rovers and made light of a distressing battle with diabetes before going on to a magnificent career with Spurs and winning 16 caps for England; rather it is to recognise the extent of a remarkable achievement.

The secret of his initial success was a phenomenal commitment to becoming a footballer. His father Ray, the former Eastville stalwart, instilled the twin ethics of competition and dedication into Gary and his elder brother, Kevin, from an early age. The latter, who went on to play for Bristol City and Crystal Palace, was always seen as the more gifted, the more likely to reach the top; but Gary had an appetite for the game which was second to none.

When he first forced his way to the fringe of Rovers' senior side in the winter of 1978, the junior member of Bristol's most famous footballing family was a leggy, colt-like teenager who was still some way from attaining his adult strength. Though his ball skills were average and he had limited pace, Gary boasted a spring-heeled leap, the result of constant practice, and read the game shrewdly.

Throughout much of his time at Eastville there was hot debate about the most effective way to use him. He ran the gamut of both full-back berths and various midfield roles, and was even tried as a front-runner, the position in which he had gained international honours at youth level.

But manager Terry Cooper always maintained that Gary was cut out for a back-four slot alongside the centre-half, and by the end of his third, final and most distinguished full season with the club, that was where he seemed the most comfortable.

Come the close of the 1981/82 campaign – with precious experience now added to his irrepressible enthusiasm and with his diabetes, diagnosed two years earlier, under control – Gary was ready to step out of the Third Division and into the First.

Newly promoted Luton were keen to sign him, but Tottenham Hotspur stepped in with a cheque for £105,000, and he was off to White Hart Lane. Thereafter he proved himself a polished performer in the top flight, rising to become captain of Spurs, and he richly deserved to wear his country's shirt on 16 occasions.

There followed an MBE for his services to the game he graced as a player for nearly two decades. Gary Mabbutt was never anything less than an impeccable ambassador for football, and a manager's dream.

RAY MABBUTT

1957/58 — 1968/69

WHEN ALL THE OTHER PLAYERS had finished training and had disappeared to back garden, business or billiard hall, the young Ray Mabbutt would attach a ball to a piece of string and hang it from the nearest convenient ceiling. Then the dapper little man with a burning desire to make the grade as a professional footballer would leap up to head it, again and again, until he was satisfied that his technique was improving. Eventually there was scarcely a more effective aerial competitor at the club.

The dedication demanded to polish that one skill typified the single-minded approach that ultimately transformed a distinctly average performer into one of the most consistent wing-halves Bristol Rovers ever had.

It was a notable achievement, not least because Ray was a late starter as a half-back. He had joined the Pirates as an inside-forward and had already made his senior debut on the wing when he was switched to left-half in the reserves. His neat and nimble style was tailored for the job and soon he earned promotion to succceed the ageing Peter Sampson.

Not abundantly endowed with natural talent, Ray scurried and hustled, often excelling as a tenacious one-on-one marker if the opposition boasted a midfield danger-man; on difficult surfaces he was particularly prominent, seeming to skate over mud and ice while those around him floundered.

His versatility was another prime asset, and he played in every position but centre-half, the stint in goal coming against Middlesbrough on New Year's Eve in 1966, after 'keeper Bernard Hall received the head injury that ended his career. The following autumn Ray staggered everyone when, as an emergency centre-forward, he scored six goals in three games, including a hat-trick at Northampton.

On attaining veteran status, in years if not in outlook, he moved on to Newport County before embarking on a lengthy tour of non-League clubs that kept him active in a respectably high grade of football until he was past 40.

Intelligent and a confirmed workaholic, Ray was not one to squander his hours away from the game. When not grooming sons Kevin and Gary for soccer stardom, he flourished in insurance and was the man who introduced Bristol to unit trusts.

Ray Mabbutt always maintained that anything was possible through hard work, and that age was a state of mind. His own life story offers eloquent evidence to support both theories.

BORN: Aylesbury, Buckinghamshire, 13.3.36

ROVERS RECORD:

League: 392 (3) games, 27 goals

FA Cup: 26 (1) games, 1 goal

League Cup: 19 games, 0 goals

Total: 437 (4) games, 28 goals

OTHER CLUBS:

Newport County 69/70-70/1 (44, 14)

NIGEL MARTYN

THERE WAS ONCE a very ordinary schoolboy winger who gave up football at the age of 16 because he suffered from asthma. A season later, as a favour to his brother, he turned out between the posts in a local works team. The former flankman enjoyed himself, played a few more games and then graduated to a neighbouring village side. Several years later, after a couple of seasons with Bristol Rovers, that same young man became Britain's first £1 million goalkeeper. Such is the story of Nigel Martyn and at the time of writing, some two decades after he entered the professional game, an ending is not in sight.

Those who watched Nigel regularly during his Twerton Park days have not been surprised at anything the big, amiable Cornishman has achieved in his subsequent career with Crystal Palace, Leeds United, Everton and England. From the moment Gerry Francis offered him a contract as he walked off the pitch after his trial in a friendly game, he scarcely put a foot or a hand wrong.

Martyn's meteoric progress as a Pirate began when senior custodian Timmy Carter was injured at the start of the 1987/88 campaign. The rookie stepped up for a supremely confident debut in a 3-1 home win over Rotherham – his proud family travelled en masse from the far West for his big day – and, apart from one short spell during which Francis worked on few finer points of technique, he was in the side for keeps.

There were no obvious flaws in Nigel's game: he was brave and athletic, caught the ball cleanly, had brilliant reflexes, and was blessed with a placid, down-to-earth temperament which success has never changed. Also he was a very quick learner who was not likely to make the same mistake twice, although one initial idiosyncrasy took a little ironing out. As a youthful custodian he had a heart-stopping habit of reaching across to make left-sided saves with his right hand – royally entertaining for the fans, but hardly conducive to managerial peace of mind.

On the strength of his first season Nigel claimed a regular England under-21 spot, and in his second he starred in Rovers' promotion bid, which foundered only at the play-off stage. Gerry Francis would have it that, even at £1 million, Crystal Palace got their man on the cheap when he moved to Selhurst Park in November 1989, and the 23-year-old's form in helping his new club reach Wembley six months later bore out that opinion.

Nigel Martyn had about him that certain aura of imperturbable confidence exuded by all the top goalkeepers, and a bolder manager of the national team would have taken him to Italy in the 1990 World Cup party. His fans back in Bristol believed that his time as England's long-term number-one would surely come, and although the timeless excellence of David Seaman curtailed his total of caps, he served his country expertly and loyally over a span of ten years. Not bad for a one-time wheezing winger . . .

BORN: St Austell, Cornwall, 11.8.66

ROVERS RECORD:

League: 101 games, 0 goals

FA Cup: 6 games, 0 goals

League Cup: 6 games, 0 goals

Others: 11 games, 0 goals

Total: 124 games, 0 goals

ROVERS HONOURS:

Third Division Championship 89/90

OTHER CLUBS:

Crystal Palace 89/90-95/6 (272, 0)

Leeds United 96/7-02/03 (207, 0)

Everton 03/04- (66,0)

23 England caps (3 won with Crystal Palace, 20 with Leeds United) 1992-2002

BORN: Camberley, Surrey, 29.10.67

ROVERS RECORD:

League: 195 (27) games, 63 goals

FA Cup: 8 (1) games, 1 goal

League Cup: 11 games, 2 goals

Others: 16 (3) games, 4 goals

Total: 230 (31) games, 70 goals

ROVERS HONOURS:

Third Division Championship 89/90

Leyland Daf Cup Finalist 89/90

OTHER CLUBS:

Exeter City (on loan) 93/4 (7, 0)

Walsall 94/5 (13, 0)

DAVID MEHEW

1985/86 — 1992/93

THEY CALLED HIM A MISFIT, they said he couldn't play; but David Mehew chose the best possible way to confound the pundits who had written him off – by finishing Bristol Rovers' Third Division title campaign as leading marksman with 18 goals.

David arrived at Eastville in July 1985 as a youngster who was surplus to the needs of Leeds United, carrying with him the recommendation of a respected coach who reckoned this forceful striker might yet have a future in the game. Indeed, after he had notched 30 goals for the reserves in his first season as a Pirate there were grounds for reflecting that the Elland Road outfit just might have made a mistake.

Delighted with his apparent windfall, Rovers boss Bobby Gould offered David his senior breakthrough, and in 1986/87 he responded with ten goals in 20 starts, a fine return by any reckoning. But when Gerry Francis became manager he favoured a front-line partnership of Gary Penrice and Devon White, which proved so productive that there seemed little immediate hope of a Mehew comeback. The frustrated goal-scorer appeared to lose confidence and even interest, going on loan first to Bath City and then Trowbridge Town, and the critics passed their damning verdicts.

His career was at the crossroads, but the non-League encounter shocked him deeply, and a gratifying transformation began.

Inspired by Francis, who coached him intensively, and supported by such senior players as Ian Holloway, Vaughan Jones and Geoff Twentyman, he worked with new purpose to build up his fitness and reclaim his place in the side.

His chance came as an attacking right-sided midfielder who was expected to help out in defence, and he made a decent fist of it. There were still those who reckoned he lacked basic technique, but he had an undeniable instinct for goals, not scoring heavily but often popping up with an important strike, and gradually he became an integral part of the team.

Come 1989/90, 'Boris', so nicknamed for his blond, Becker-type looks, began to catch the eye. The nearer he got to goal the faster he seemed to run, bearing down on the 'keeper with his distinctive pigeon-toed gait. He found the net with increasing regularity, developing a penchant for subtle chips and lobs, the fruit of many hours spent polishing his skills. At last the one-time enigma could afford a chuckle at his detractors' expense.

Some pundits reckoned David would wither in the Second Division, but he held his own for a couple of seasons before struggling for a place in the troubled term of 1992/93, which ended in relegation. After that he managed little impact elsewhere, but at least David Mehew could be satisfied that he had made his mark during the best of times for the Pirates.

BRIAN PARKIN

BRIAN PARKIN arrived at Twerton Park in 1989 from Crystal Palace reserves to take the place of Britain's first £1 million goalkeeper and was promptly handed Nigel Martyn's tattered old training kit. If they'd had the same foot size, Parkin might literally have stepped into Martyn's boots, such was the emphasis on thrift during Rovers' exile at Twerton Park.

Thus it was that one of the club's most colourful characters began a distinguished career with the Pirates that earned him a Division Three Championship medal in 1989/90 and saw him make two trips to Wembley to face Tranmere Rovers in the 1990 Leyland Daf Cup Final and Huddersfield Town in the 1995 Division Two play-off final.

When Parkin rejoined the club in 1999 to enjoy a handful of senior outings, he claimed the post-war record for a Rovers goalkeeper by overtaking Howard Radford by one game, the Merseysider stretching his League total to 246 appearances. Brian might have played even more games for the club had he not been one of the players who approached the board in 1993 to air concerns over Malcolm Allison's managerial style. News of the delegation reached Big Mal and the 'keeper spent most of the remainder of the season on the bench.

Parkin never gave the impression of being unduly burdened by a respect for authority, a trait which endeared him to the fans, yet he was a dedicated professional who organised his defence with authority, often with a few well-aimed expletives thrown in. He was far more than a shot-stopper, and anyone who suggests to him that reaction saves were his main strength runs the risk of a blunt rebuttal of such an ill-informed opinion. Certainly, when Parkin was in his prime he was an accomplished all-round performer and could lay a justifiable claim to being the best English goalkeeper outside the top division.

Although he might have given the impression of being an off-the-cuff character in the great Rovers adventure, Parkin prepared meticulously for games. He felt he didn't do himself justice in that first Wembley appearance against Tranmere and before the Huddersfield game he spent 25 minutes with his own thoughts in the dressing room while the rest of the team walked around the Wembley pitch in the sunshine.

Brian brought a high level of intensity to his game and at his best he was able to combine immense determination with ability, bravery and the splash of eccentricity with which many of the greatest custodians are blessed.

Parkin left for Wycombe Wanderers in 1996, but was brought back to Bristol by Ian Holloway in 1999 as cover for Lee Jones, and he started his last game for the club against Cardiff at the end of the 1999/2000 campaign. Rovers had to win to make the play-offs – having seemed certainties for automatic promotion earlier in the season – and it was an unusual gamble to replace the goalkeeper for such an important game. Although Rovers famously lost 1-0 at Ninian Park, undoubtedly their most committed player that day was Brian Parkin.

BORN: Birkenhead, Cheshire, 12.10.65

ROVERS RECORD:

League: 243 (3) games, 0 goals

FA Cup: 12 games, 0 goals

League Cup: 11 games, 0 goals

Others: 24 games, 0 goals

Total: 290 (3) games, 0 goals

ROVERS HONOURS:

Third Division Championship 89/90

Leyland Daf Cup Finalist 89/90

OTHER CLUBS:

Oldham Athletic 83/4-84/5 (6, 0)

Crewe Alexandra 84/5-87/8 (98, 0)

Crystal Palace 88/9-89/90 (20, 0)

Wycombe Wanderers 96/7-98/9 (26, 0)

Notts County 98/9 (1, 0)

BORN: Bristol, 20.3.46

ROVERS RECORD:

League: 354 (5) games, 0 goals

FA Cup: 28 games, 0 goals

League Cup: 27 (1) games, 0 goals

Others: 5 games, 0 goals

Total: 414 (6) games, 0 goals

ROVERS HONOURS:

Promotion from Division Three 73/4

Watney Cup 72/3

OTHER CLUBS:

Torquay United 77/8-78/9 (56, 0)

LINDSAY PARSONS

1963/64 — 1976/77

PUT ANY BRISTOL ROVERS PLAYER of the Dodgin-Megson era on the spot by asking him to name the man he would choose to stand beside him in a fight for his life, and the chances are that he'd nominate Lindsay Parsons.

The indomitable defender, who once played in a double-century of consecutive matches and went on to make more appearances for the Pirates than any other left-back in their history, received precious little public acclaim. But the recognition that matters most – that of the men who shared a dressing room with him for 15 years – spoke volumes about as brave and loyal a campaigner as Eastville has seen.

Lindsay, who made his debut as an 18-year-old in 1964 but didn't become a regular for another six years, always played to his strengths. He was exceedingly quick, tackled powerfully, covered his colleagues well and hated to be beaten in the air, but he would never claim to be an artist with the ball. Accordingly, his game was to win possession and pass to the nearest colleague with a minimum of fuss.

A right-footer despite almost invariably playing on the left, Lindsay was at his most comfortable against strong, direct attackers, sometimes struggling to cope with wilier, jinking opponents. One trickster he relished facing, however, was Willie Morgan, whom he tamed in four confrontations, two each with Manchester United and Bolton, though he owns up to a runaround from the Scot in one defeat at Old Trafford.

There were those who criticised Lindsay for not getting forward more, reckoning that anyone with his pace should have been a dangerous overlapper. But perhaps he lacked a little confidence, especially as a youngster, and preferred to slip the ball to his winger, enjoying a particularly productive partnership with Colin Dobson in 1973/74.

Had he crossed the half-way line more often, Lindsay would surely have improved his goal tally – or, to be more accurate, acquired one. The records state that he failed to score in each of his 420 senior outings, but it's a statistic with which he takes grave issue. To this day he maintains good-humouredly that his 20-yard drive in a 1971 FA Cup-tie against Cambridge at Eastville entered the net without Bruce Bannister getting a touch, although the jaunty little striker claimed the credit.

With or without that goal Lindsay, who went on to work for Rolls-Royce while relishing his football as a manager in non-League circles, and also served a stint as number-two to Tony Pulis at Bristol City, will go down as one of the most consistent performers ever to wear the blue-and-white quarters.

GARY PENRICE

1984/85 — 1989/90 & 1997/98 — 1999/2000

GARY PENRICE proved in his first spell as a Pirate that he could be more than a little useful in the second flight of the English game, and hinted at his potential to grace the top echelon. In the third grade, where he spent five formative years honing his talents with Bristol Rovers, he was downright extraordinary.

The dark, dapper Bristolian could do things on a football pitch that no visitor to Eastville or Twerton Park might reasonably expect to see in the lower reaches of the Football League. He could receive the ball from any angle and control it instantly, deceive defenders with the most subtle of distribution and score goals that would not have been out of place at any level.

Yet despite his unquestionable skill, Gary was rejected as a youngster by both Bristol clubs for being too small and frail, and it was with Mangotsfield United that he first came to local prominence. After attracting the attention of Rovers boss David Williams with a string of scintillating Western League displays, he enlisted at Eastville as a striker of great promise.

But when Bobby Gould took over as manager in the summer of 1985, he saw the Penrice flair and creativity as qualities needed desperately in midfield, and the confident front-man was withdrawn to a deep position. Gary was an enigma in his new role, outstanding in one game, almost inept in his next. His exciting potential was always in evidence, but there were times when he ran himself and the team into trouble by taking on too many opponents.

The turning point in his career was the arrival of Gerry Francis to replace Gould in July 1987. One of the former England captain's first moves was to push Gary forward, where he could give full rein to his trickery and vision without putting the side under pressure if the ball was lost. Paired with the gargantuan Devon White, he was a revelation. As well as scoring freely, Gary could retain possession in tight spaces, bravely shielding the ball and revealing a wiry strength that belied his physical stature.

He played a major part in Rovers' progress to the 1989 Third Division play-offs, in which his 30-yard dipper against Port Vale at Twerton Park was a spectacular strike even by his standards. Early in the next season he accepted a £500,000 move to Second Division Watford, where he was an instant hit, then stuttered in a brief stint with Aston Villa before exhibiting Premiership quality with Queen's Park Rangers.

In July 1997, following a second stop-off at Vicarage Road and by now aged 33, he returned to Rovers and sparkled anew. Gary's guile, and his ability to hold the ball before using it to thoughtful advantage, was a major factor reaching that term's play-offs. Over the next two campaigns he took on a lower-key playing role, but became immensely influential as coach and assistant manager to Ian Holloway, then Gary left Rovers for Queen's Park Rangers with his boss in 2000/01, taking the post of first team coach.

BORN: Bristol, 23.3.64

ROVERS RECORD:

League: 234 (23) games, 60 goals

FA Cup: 18 (4) games, 9 goals

League Cup: 13 (1) games, 3 goals

Others: 16 (2) games, 3 goals

Total: 281 (30) games, 75 goals

OTHER CLUBS:

Watford 89/90-90/1 (43, 17)

Aston Villa 90/1-91/2 (20, 1)

Queen's Park Rangers 91/2-95/6 (82, 20)

Watford 95/6-96/7 (39, 2)

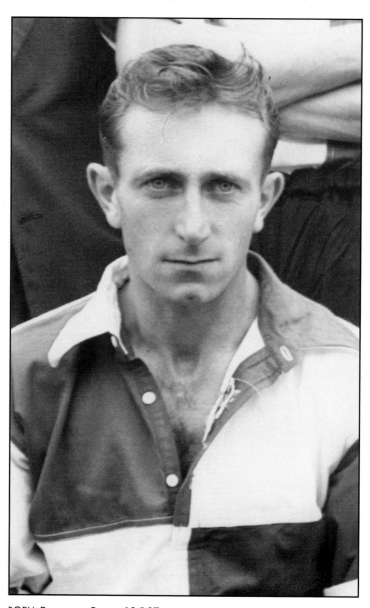

BORN: Devonport, Devon, 19.5.27

ROVERS RECORD:

League: 452 games, 85 goals

FA Cup: 40 games, 7 goals

League Cup: 4 games, 0 goals

Total: 496 games, 92 goals

ROVERS HONOURS:

Division Three South Championship 52/3

GEORGE PETHERBRIDGE

1946/47 — 1961/62

IF YOU STAND just 5ft 4in in your stockinged feet and want to make your living as a professional footballer, then you have to be rather special. George Petherbridge was all of that, and then some.

'Winky Pop', who somehow always had the superficial appearance of a little old man – an impression dispelled rapidly when he started to play – served the Rovers loyally and with distinction from the end of the war until the early 1960s. He plied his entertaining trade with equal dexterity on either wing, switching readily from his usual right flank whenever it suited the side, and such was his consistency that he was the only player in the Football League to score for the same club in each of the 16 seasons spanned by his career.

George was irrepressibly enthusiastic about the game, and the effervescent outlook shone through his every act on the field. His dainty footwork, crossing skills and deceptively fierce shot for one so slight were beloved of the Eastville faithful. They identified with the indomitable spirit he took into confrontations with the most physical of opponents, many of whom were so many sizes bigger than him that they might have hailed from another planet.

The diminutive Devonian, an adoptive Bristolian from the age of three, joined his one and only League club after being rejected by Arsenal. Rovers boss Brough Fletcher was adamant that lack of inches was no bar to success, and after two seasons of intermittent first-team appearances George laid unarguable claim to a regular berth.

Soon he became one of the Pirates' principal creators, though it was his knack of cutting inside his full-back to make chances for himself that made the headlines in December 1951, when he shocked Torquay United with a four-goal salvo at Eastville.

George went on to play an influential part in taking the Third Division South title in 1952/53, and after another nine consistent years it was entirely unfitting that his last campaign, during which he worked selflessly on the development of his replacement Harold Jarman, should end in relegation.

After leaving Rovers he ran a pub, worked as sports master at Millfield School, managed Western League Glastonbury and played cricket, his second great sporting love, as often as possible. In later years he became head groundsman at Wells Cathedral School, where any youngster with sporting ambitions could not have wished for a more inspiring role model than George Petherbridge.

BORN: Willenhall, Staffordshire, 20.5.20

DIED: Bristol, 17.8.04

ROVERS RECORD:

League: 467 games, 16 goals

FA Cup: 35 games, 2 goals

Total: 502 games, 18 goals

ROVERS HONOURS:

Third Division South Championship 52/3

JACKIE PITT

1946/47 — 1957/58

WHEN JACKIE PITT reached the wrong side of 50 he could still chip a football with more precision than the average modern professional – and that was wearing his Wellington boots! So just how good was he in his Second Division prime, when Bristol Rovers never finished lower than tenth in the table and no visiting team relished a visit to Eastville?

Quite simply, Jackie was a class act, a right-half of vision, skill and power who had all the attributes demanded of a performer at the highest club level. Bert Tann, manager during that most successful spell in the Pirates' history and a man notoriously thrifty with his plaudits, reckoned the wiry Midlander should have played for England.

That he never progressed into the top flight was more a comment on the times than his abilities. In Pitt's day players were condemned to receive a maximum wage, so the possibility of a lucrative transfer to a prosperous club was not an issue; in keeping with this spirit, Rovers operated a strict policy of no-buy-no-sell.

Not that Jackie was unhappy to spend his entire career in the famous blue-and-white quarters. He was possessed of a genuine love for the Rovers, which became apparent to any who faced him on the field. He could tackle like a steel-sprung mantrap and was particularly venomous when it came to protecting diminutive right-winger George Petherbridge from the over-zealous attentions of hulking full-backs. His physical battles with Bristol City's equally enthusiastic Ernie Peacock perfectly exemplified his commitment, and the clash which ended with the pair of them being sent off has passed into Bristol soccer folklore.

But for all his ardour, it is for sheer talent on the ball that Jackie Pitt deserves to be remembered. His passing and control were immaculate, whether in defensive tandem with right-back Harry Bamford or pressing forward to create goal-scoring chances for Geoff Bradford and Vic Lambden, who fed voraciously off a staple diet of his teasingly clipped crosses.

Jackie, who became skipper when Ray Warren retired, went on to coach under Bert Tann, but that was one job to which this most loyal and unassuming of men was not suited. Instead he became groundsman, first at Eastville and then at Twerton Park. In Bath, having reached his seventies with his characteristic vitality gloriously intact, he continued to serve the club he graced as a player of rare polish and passion.

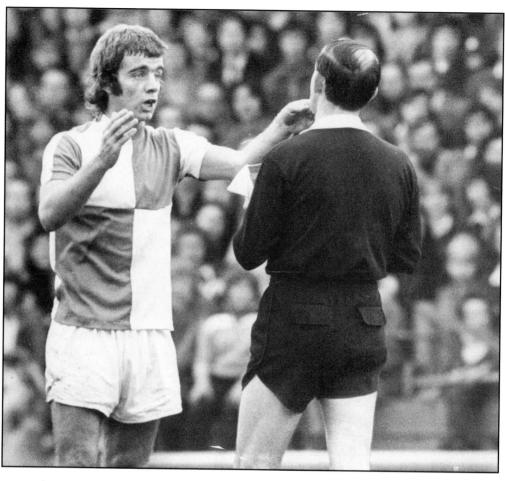

BORN: Penarth, Glamorgan, 1.12.49

ROVERS RECORD:

League: 360 (2) games, 22 goals

FA Cup: 20 (1) games, 1 goal

League Cup: 28 games, 2 goals

Others: 8 games, 1 goal

Total: 416 (3) games, 26 goals

ROVERS HONOURS:

Promotion from Third Division 73/4

Watney Cup 72/3

OTHER CLUBS:

Exeter City 80/1-81/2 (31, 2)

FRANKIE PRINCE

1967/68 — 1979/80

NO OBSTACLE was too high, no task too great for Frankie Prince. Whatever the challenge he would give it a go. If his mentor, Bill Dodgin, had asked him to take on George Best and Bobby Charlton single-handed – oh, and Denis Law too, while he was about it – he would have rolled up his sleeves and got on with the job.

Frankie was Rovers' ball-winner-in-chief for more than a decade, and especially in the early years, with his skinhead hair-do a fitting badge of office, he was a fearsome proposition. It had not always been so.

On arrival from the Pirates' South Wales nursery he was a light, almost frail youngster with matchstick legs who appeared hardly capable of kicking a football, let alone going on to earn a reputation as one of the hardest tacklers in the lower divisions.

But Frankie wanted to be a player, and he worked hard to become one. Spurred on by Dodgin, who admired the dedication of the wiry midfielder, he made his senior debut at 18, was a Rovers' regular before his 21st birthday and was on the bench for a full international two years later; unhappily, he never did win a cap above under-23 level.

In those early years, when his edges were not so much rough as serrated, Frankie tended at times to commit himself rashly, and some of his clashes with City's Gerry Gow, in particular, were strictly X-rated. But as he matured his style became less frenetic and more effective.

His image as a hard man – Don Megson dubbed him his Sherman tank during the 1973/74 promotion term – was heightened by his vocal approach on the field. But there was a constructive side to his game which was not always appreciated by the casual observer. After gaining possession, Frankie would side-foot the ball to a team-mate before moving instantly to support him, and from such a basic ploy, in the 1972 Watney Cup tie with Burnley at Turf Moor, came one of Rovers' slickest goals of the decade.

The Welshman laid the ball off in his own half, sprinted forward as Brian Godfrey and Bruce Bannister interchanged passes, and arrived on the edge of the box to score with a precise low drive.

Never the quickest of players, Frankie compensated by reading the game astutely, a quality which served him well during a central-defensive stint alongside Stuart Taylor in 1976/77. By then he had confounded the doubters who had predicted he hadn't the class to survive in the Second Division. He was, in fact, a model professional, a serious and thorough young man who never gave less than his best. Who could ask for more?

BORN: Wolverhampton, Staffordshire,
27.5.72

ROVERS RECORD:

League: 157 (6) games, 1 goal

FA Cup: 12 (1) games, 0 goals

League Cup: 11 games, 0 goals

Others: 10 (1) games, 0 goals

Total: 190 (8) games, 1 goal

OTHER CLUBS:

West Bromwich Albion 91/2 (5, 0)

DAVID PRITCHARD

1993/94 — 2001/02

IT'S ONE OF THE ODDITIES of football that sometimes the most competitive players on the pitch are the most relaxed characters away from the game. That was certainly the case with David Pritchard, whose tenacious displays earned him the nickname 'Pitbull' among his team-mates. Off the field, meanwhile, the boy from the Black Country was a remarkably easy-going individual with a reputation as a wheeler-dealer, and a mad-keen Wolves fan whose father was chief steward at Molineux.

Rovers goalkeeper Brian Parkin rates Pritch as the bravest player he's ever seen and the fans quickly appreciated his willingness to launch himself into tackles without a second thought for his personal well-being.

David arrived at Twerton Park from Telford United in 1993 to replace right-back Ian Alexander, the last survivor of Gerry Francis's formidable promotion-winning defence. By then Rovers had been relegated to Division Two following the troubled reigns of Martin Dobson, Dennis Rofe and Malcolm Allison, but new manager John Ward built his own impressive back-line of Parkin, Pritchard, Andy Tillson, Billy Clark and Andy Gurney. It was on this solid platform that he based the promotion challenge of 1994/95 which ended in play-off final defeat against Huddersfield Town at Wembley.

If Pritchard had remained at right-back he might never have achieved the cult status accorded him by the supporters – it was not until player-boss Ian Holloway moved him into midfield that his exceptional bravery and commitment became fully evident.

The Rovers faithful have spent many long hours pondering why Holloway's team collected only six points from the final ten games of the 1999/2000 season and missed the play-offs by one place. Most identify a collective anxiety as the cause, but some remember the January visit to Colchester as a turning point. Rovers lost 5-4 after being 3-1 ahead and, significantly, just after half-time Pritch was seriously injured in a challenge with Titus Bramble. He didn't play again that term, and when Ronnie Mauge broke his leg playing for Trinidad and Tobago a month later, the Rovers midfield became a far less daunting unit.

Pritch was still on crutches when Rovers lost calamitously at Cardiff on the final day, and although his presence in the side might not have changed the result, it would almost certainly have altered the nature of the performance. He would never have allowed his team-mates to have played so tentatively – even its owner keeps a wary eye on a 'Pitbull'.

Famously, David didn't score many goals. In fact, he managed one. But it will always be remembered because Rovers fan Ben Davies kept his promise to walk back to Bristol from the ground at which Pritch scored his first goal. As it turned out, Ben got off reasonably lightly with a 154-mile hike from Chesterfield.

Pritchard never fully recovered from his fateful injury at Layer Road and after a brief appearance in 2001/02 he retired to pursue business interests in Spain.

PHIL PURNELL

1985/86 — 1991/92

PHIL PURNELL is one of the few men to have experienced the complete spectrum of emotions the club endured and enjoyed between 1986 and 1990. The affable Bristolian played in the last-ever game at Eastville, a 1-1 draw against Chesterfield in April 1986; he scored the goal against Newport County that guaranteed Rovers Third Division survival in May 1987; he was in the team that thrashed Bristol City 3-0 to win promotion three years later, and he scored against Blackpool in the subsequent victory that crowned the Pirates as champions.

The only others to appear in the Eastville swansong, then survive to earn a title medal in 1990 were Vaughan Jones and Gary Penrice. Jones, like Purnell, seemed to have lost his chance to pursue a professional career some years earlier, and Penrice, again like Purnell, rose through the non-League ranks at Mangotsfield United to become a Bristol Rovers great.

The enduring image of Phil Purnell is of a lean, tousled-haired left-winger, skipping past opponents in front of his vociferous fan-base in the Twerton 'Shed' and swinging in crosses towards the imposing figure of Devon White.

Phil played as if he didn't have a care in the world. From the terraces he was viewed as a man of the people, a Rovers fan who gave everything for the cause and provided much of the flair in Gerry Francis's meticulously organised side.

David Mehew was the right-sided midfielder who tended to cut in from the flank, whereas Purnell was at his most effective using his pace in the channel two yards in from the left touchline, often to chase a Geoff Twentyman pass up the famous Twerton slope.

Although Purnell originally signed for Rovers as a schoolboy, a series of injuries seemed to end his hopes of becoming a professional. Duly he took a three-year apprenticeship at British Aerospace and worked with his father selling furniture, but all the time he was beavering his way back to fitness and catching the eye with his performances for Mangotsfield. It was a fitting reward that the effort Phil put in at Cossham Street would see him not only help Rovers to promotion, but also play at Wembley in the 1990 Leyland Daf Cup Final against Tranmere Rovers.

There was genuine camaraderie in the small Rovers squad assembled mainly from apprentices, cast-offs and non-League players, and 'Percy', along with Ian Holloway, Gary Penrice and Steve Yates, brought a distinctly Bristolian character to a side that Gerry Francis had organised and motivated to perform so far above expectations.

Phil Purnell seemed destined to enjoy a long career with Rovers, or even to move up a division, such was his talent. Sadly, he never fully recovered from yet another injury and left the professional game to concentrate on playing cricket for his beloved Winterbourne. Phil went on to become a football agent, with Marcus Stewart among the players on his books.

BORN: Bristol, 16.9.64

ROVERS RECORD:

League: 130 (23) games, 22 goals

FA Cup: 7 (1) games, 0 goals

League Cup: 6 (2) games, 0 goals

Others: 17 (1) games, 0 goals

Total: 160 (27 games), 22 goals

ROVERS HONOURS:

Third Division Championship 89/90

Leyland Daf Cup Finalist 89/90

OTHER CLUBS:

Swansea City (on loan) 91/2 (5, 1)

BORN: Liverpool, 16.2.58

ROVERS RECORD:

League: 218 (19) games, 94 goals

FA Cup: 12 (1) games, 4 goals

League Cup: 19 (1) games, 7 goals

Others: 6 (1) games, 1 goal

Total: 255 (22) games, 106 goals

OTHER CLUBS:

Stoke City 78/9-80/1 (46, 7)

PAUL RANDALL

1977/78 — 1978/79 & 1980/81 — 1985/86

RARELY DID A PLAYER win a place in the hearts of the Eastville faithful more quickly and with more downright panache than Paul Randall in the late 1970s. The glory days of Warboys and Bannister were over and the Rovers attack was wearing a distinctly impoverished look when young Paul left his job with a Glastonbury supermarket to become the Pirates' new scoring messiah.

Slight, boyish and a natural footballer, he excited and charmed the fans with his unorthodox touches and instinctive strikes, and his 20 goals in 28 outings staved off relegation to the Third Division in 1977/78.

It was an eye-catching display to knock much-fancied Southampton out of that season's FA Cup that turned him into a national figure. Paul scored both goals in a 2-0 victory, delicately chipping the first, dancing through the defence to slot home the second, and a transfer to a more fashionable club was inevitable.

It was easy to see why the talent scouts were flocking to Eastville. Rovers' slimline predator was exceptionally fast, had an eye for the slightest opening and was blessed with clinical finishing ability. He revelled in one-on-one confrontations with 'keepers, having the precious, intuitive knack of dispatching the ball at the optimum moment.

Unhappily for Paul, when his big move came along it was the wrong one. After a prolific start to the new campaign he joined Stoke City for £175,000 in December 1978, much to the dismay of his legion of supporters, and quickly helped the Potters into the First Division. But he failed to do himself justice in the top grade, and in January 1981 Terry Cooper brought him back to bottom-of-the-table Rovers for £55,000.

With their hero restored, the fans were ecstatic, believing he would prove to be a saviour once again. He didn't, the Pirates went down and, although Paul performed adequately for five more years, he never recaptured his Midas touch.

He always had critics who wanted him to work harder but, if he gave the impression of being lackadaisical, it was a false one. Paul was a specialist who applied all his energies to his sole objective of finding the net, and when a chance was in the offing there was no shortage of effort.

In March 1986, aged only 28, he was released by Bobby Gould. Apparently lacking ambition, he joined first Yeovil Town and then Bath City, scoring heavily for both. It seemed a lamentably premature departure from League football by a player who still had much to offer.

ANDY REECE

1987/88 — 1992/93

WHEN GERRY FRANCIS guided Bristol Rovers to the Championship of Division Three and to a Wembley final in 1990, he enjoyed that vital element of good fortune with injuries and suspensions that enabled him to pick a settled team throughout the season. Geoff Twentyman, Vaughan Jones, Steve Yates and Ian Holloway played in every game, while Andy Reece missed just three starts.

Midlander Reece was a vital cog in the Rovers promotion plan and immeasurably more important to the success of the side than can be gleaned from statistics alone. He arrived at Twerton Park from Dudley Town and in doing so joined a prestigious roll of honour made up of players from a non-League background who have achieved mightily with Bristol Rovers.

Reece was the perfect central midfield foil to Holloway in that triumphant combination. Although Bristolian 'Ollie' grabbed plenty of attention with his obvious passion for the club, Andy was the deep-lying prompter blessed with the knack of dispensing pinpoint passes, the unsung hero who patrolled the area in front of the defence with ruthless, cool efficiency. For all his self-possession, though, let no one doubt that Reece was just as passionate about Bristol Rovers as any of his comrades.

The Gerry Francis side was superbly organised and the unflappable Salopian was one of the individuals vital to the manager's method. In all honesty it didn't always produce the most attractive brand of football, but undoubtedly it produced results. Accordingly Rovers were unbeaten at home for the first time in their history in 1989/90, arguably the greatest season the club has ever known.

Reece was a key component of the team that played for the first time at Wembley when they reached the Leyland Daf Cup Final, but lost 2-1 to Tranmere Rovers. But even that crushing disappointment couldn't detract from the dramatic climax of the League campaign a few weeks earlier when Bristol City visited Twerton Park on the evening of May 2nd 1990 for the Pirates' final home game of the season. If City won they would be promoted as Champions while a draw would also be enough to see the Ashton Gate team go up. A victory for Rovers would guarantee promotion and keep alive their chances of being crowned Division Three Champions.

Unforgettably, Rovers thrashed their neighbours 3-0, with Reece playing a typical precision pass from deep in his own half in the build-up to Devon White's opening goal. The post-match celebrations on the Twerton pitch that evening, with Andy leading the singing from the stand, captured a perfect moment in the Rovers story. City had been humiliated and denied promotion, Rovers were promoted. Rovers went on to take the title with a 3-0 victory at Blackpool, while City went up in second place.

Andy Reece will long be remembered for his inspirational rather than sensational role in Rovers' finest hour. He stayed at the club until 1993, when he joined Hereford United before taking up a career with the West Midlands Constabulary.

Born: Shrewsbury, Shropshire, 5.9.62

ROVERS RECORD:

League: 230 (9) games, 17 goals

FA Cup: 10 (2) games, 3 goals

League Cup: 11 (1) games, 0 goals

Others: 21 games, 3 goals

Total: 272 (12) games, 23 goals

ROVERS HONOURS:

Third Division Championship 89/90

Leyland Daf Cup Finalist 89/90

OTHER CLUBS:

Walsall (on loan) 92/3 and 93/4 (15, 1)

Hereford United 93/4-95/6 (71, 5)

JASON ROBERTS

CONFIDENCE CAN BE AS IMPORTANT an asset as skill and hard graft in a successful football team. In his prime Jason Roberts played with a swagger bordering on arrogance, and that was never more vividly in evidence than when he found himself racing towards goal with only the 'keeper to beat. If you had to pick one Rovers player of modern times who would invariably score in a one-on-one scenario, probably it would be Paul Randall. If you had to pick another, it would have to be Jason Roberts.

Ian Holloway first spotted Roberts when he was a raw but powerful performer with non-League Hayes. The Rovers boss tried to buy the rookie marksman at that point, but he moved to Wolverhampton Wanderers. However, he failed to break into the first team at Molineux, joining Torquay, then Bristol City on loan before Holloway finally took him to The Memorial Stadium in August 1998 for a fee of £250,000.

Roberts began the 1998/99 campaign playing alongside Jamie Cureton and Barry Hayles in an adventurous attacking formation. But it wasn't until the departure of Hayles to Fulham in November 1998 that Rovers fans saw the best of Jason Roberts as he formed a prolific partnership with Jamie Cureton, the pair contributing 93 goals in all competitions over two seasons.

Power and pace were the twin hallmarks of Jason's game, attributes he had developed in the rough-and-tumble of non-League football. He relished a good old-fashioned scrap with the opposition centre-half although he had a tendency to go to ground rather too easily in his early games. Gary Penrice must take much of the credit for grooming Roberts into such an accomplished striker; having identified the Grenadian's strengths, 'Penny' worked tirelessly on building the self-belief that was perhaps lacking when the youngster arrived at The Memorial Stadium.

Roberts was never a player to give the referee an easy afternoon if he felt he wasn't getting his fair share of the free-kicks his style of play tended to generate. But he was never less than an impeccable professional, as might be expected from a lad who hails from a distinguished sporting family. Among his uncles are former England international striker Cyrille Regis; Dave Regis, who played more than 150 games in the lower divisions, and Otis Roberts, a professional footballer in Hong Kong and Belgium, while Olympic athlete John Regis is a cousin.

Given his dynamism, commitment and goal-scoring prowess, it's a shame that Roberts' final game for Rovers was the insipid 1-0 defeat at Cardiff which meant missing out on the 1999/2000 promotion play-offs.

He left The Memorial Stadium to join Cyrille Regis' former club, West Bromwich Albion, for £2 million, and served them in the Premiership in 2002/03 before playing a handful of top-flight matches for Portsmouth in 2003/04. After that he joined Wigan, where he formed a productive partnership with his former Rovers protégé Nathan Ellington, a major factor in the Latics' rise to join the elite in 2005.

BORN: Park Royal, Grenada, 25.1.78

ROVERS RECORD:

League: 73 (5) games, 38 goals

FA Cup: 6 games, 7 goals

League Cup: 6 games, 3 goals

Others: 3 games, 0 goals

Total: 88 (5) games, 48 goals

OTHER CLUBS:

Wolverhampton Wanderers 97/8 (0, 0)

Torquay United on loan 97/8 (14, 6)

Bristol City on loan 97/8 (3, 1)

West Bromwich Albion 00/01-03/04 (89, 24)

Portsmouth on loan 03/04 (10, 1)

Wigan Athletic 03/04- (59, 29)

Grenada caps

BORN: Cardiff, 24.2.50

ROVERS RECORD:

League: 174 (1) games, 6 goals

FA Cup: 9 games, 0 goals

League Cup: 19 games, 1 goal

Others: 3 games, 0 goals

Total: 205 (1) games, 7 goals

ROVERS HONOURS:

Watney Cup 72/3

OTHER CLUBS:

Portsmouth 73/4-77/8 (153, 1)

Hereford United 78/9 (3, 0)

Exeter City 78/9-81/2 (105, 0)

4 Wales caps (won with Portsmouth) 1974

PHIL ROBERTS

1969/70 — 1972/73

THE FIRST TIME PHIL ROBERTS bade farewell to Eastville he was heading back to Cardiff as a homesick youngster who had simply had enough of Bristol. On his second departure he left as the most expensive footballer the club had ever sold. In between, he learned his trade so well that he went on to become one of the few graduates from the Pirates' prolific South Wales nursery to win full international honours.

Phil, whose ambitions of making the grade in his native city had been hampered when he broke his leg in a schoolboy coaching session with the Ninian Park club, made rapid progress when he returned to Rovers after thinking better of his premature exit as a teenager.

A right-back who could also play in midfield or central defence, he was raw but engagingly eager to learn, a quality close to the heart of Bill Dodgin, then Rovers' chief scout and a champion of the blond rookie's cause. It was fitting that it should be Bill, this time as manager, who gave Phil his senior debut in a 5-1 victory at Reading in August 1969.

The Welshman made an immediate impact with his strength in the tackle and eye-catching speed on the overlap, soon winning a permanent place in the side.

In those early days, however, Phil was not bounteously endowed with tactical awareness, all too often being caught out of position after impetuous attacking forays, and several goals were conceded when opponents sneaked into space he should have been occupying.

Characteristically, he worked hard to correct the flaw, and was rewarded for his endeavour in December 1970 with selection for Wales's under-23 encounter with England at Wrexham. A posse of First Division scouts saw Phil excel against stars such as Mick Channon and Dave Thomas, and transfer rumours began to circulate.

The adaptable defender further enhanced his reputation ten months later with a limpet-like marking job on Rodney Marsh in two League Cup clashes with Queen's Park Rangers. Marsh did score in the first match with a spectacular free-kick, but it was the only opening he got in 180 minutes of football.

Phil, who troubled 'keepers occasionally with his long-range shooting, continued to attract national attention, and eventually he was sold to Second Division Portsmouth for £55,000 in May 1973. Four full caps followed, but the Dodgin protégé did not make the progress many had predicted, and he completed his playing days with Exeter City.

BORN: Great Watering, Essex, 9.2.27

ROVERS RECORD:

League: 339 games, 4 goals

FA Cup: 32 games, 0 goals

League Cup: 1 game, 0 goals

Total: 372 games, 4 goals

ROVERS HONOURS:

Third Division South Championship 52/3

PETER SAMPSON

1948/49 — 1960/61

PETER SAMPSON would be too modest to say it, and in all probability he has never even thought about it, but he was one of the greatest influences for good on that classic Bristol Rovers side that earned Eastville its finest hour by lifting the Third Division South title in 1952/53. Peter, who rarely caught either the eye or the imagination as he went about his business as a quietly efficient wing-half, was never known to be in a bad mood. No matter what dark cloud hung over the dressing room, he had the same lovely way with him, a genuine, unforced cheerfulness that often put matters into perspective for some of his more tempestuous colleagues.

Not that 'Sammy' was any slouch on the pitch. During the Championship campaign he was an ever-present at left-half for the third consecutive season, toiling at the heart of the side with the equally consistent Jackie Pitt to his right.

The pair complemented each other to perfection. Short-ball specialist Jackie was the more creative and adventurous partner, often moving forward to attack. Peter, who favoured longer passes, confined himself largely to defensive duties, in which his almost uncanny knack of intercepting dangerous through-balls was an inconspicuous but telling factor in the team's success.

Also Peter was blessed with an instinct for danger, and invariably it was he who would arrive to cover if a fellow defender found himself in trouble. Ever unobtrusive, he was not a man-of-the-match type of player, but two performances stand out, both against high-quality opposition. At Upton Park in March 1957 he scarcely put a foot wrong in a surprise victory against West Ham United, and ten months later he gave a courageous fighting display to help conquer Burnley at Turf Moor in a hectic FA Cup replay.

When Peter was eventually replaced by Ray Mabbutt, he could look back on a creditable career that had gathered momentum after a slow start. Having bought himself out of the Army for £65 to sign for Rovers – there had also been interest from Fulham and Bristol City – his progress had been tentative.

There had been those who had reckoned he wouldn't make the grade, but perseverance paid off for one of the nicest men ever to grace Eastville. In later years that engaging personality was enjoyed by the householders of Kingswood, where he became a milkman.

BORN: Birmingham, 26.11.64

ROVERS RECORD:

League: 123 (19) games, 42 goals

FA Cup: 7 games, 6 goals

League Cup: 3 (1) games, 0 goals

Others: 7 (2) games, 3 goals

Total: 140 (22) games, 51 goals

ROVERS HONOURS:

Third Division Championship 89/90

Leyland Daf Cup Finalist 89/90

OTHER CLUBS:

Stoke City 82/3-89/90 (164, 24)

Oxford United non-contract 93/4 (5, 0)

Walsall non-contract 93/4 (2, 0)

CARL SAUNDERS

1989/90 — 1993/94

CARL SAUNDERS was something of an oddity in the Third Division Championship and Wembley side of 1989/90 in that he'd commanded a fee, rather than arrived in the first team through the youth system or on a free transfer. At £70,000 he was, quite comfortably, the most expensive player in the squad when he was acquired from Stoke in February 1990 to replace Gary Penrice, a recent £500,000 departure to Watford.

Saunders had been a Potter in the equivalent of the Premiership before falling out of favour during a series of management changes at the old Victoria Ground, and his readiness to step down the League ladder to enlist with Rovers puzzled some observers. If the man himself were to be asked why he chose Rovers, the chances are he would give a two-word answer: Gerry Francis.

The Midlander was a natural winger or striker but also had served Stoke at full-back and in midfield, and it was this versatility that Francis coveted for his squad. Thanks maybe to his experience at a higher level, Carl fitted quickly fitted into his new surroundings and became a key component during the climax of the successful promotion campaign.

He scored on his debut and formed a partnership with Devon White reminiscent of the great 'Smash and Grab' pairing of Alan Warboys and Bruce Bannister in the 1970s. Inspired by Francis's international background and instilled with fresh confidence by the manager's renowned motivational skills, Saunders found favour with the Twerton Park fans as a skilful finisher and an unselfish provider blessed with the vision to bring his team-mates into the game.

Although he thrived on knock-downs by the formidable White, there was far more to his game than being a collector of scraps. Often Carl dropped deep to avoid his markers and it was from such a position that he thundered a goal which entered Rovers folklore, a 25-yard volley past Bruce Grobbelaar to put the Pirates ahead in an FA Cup replay against Liverpool at Anfield. In the previous round he had scored four times in the 5-0 home defeat of Plymouth Argyle, the first time that a Rovers man had contributed an FA Cup quartet since 'Cannonball' Jack Jones plundered five against Weymouth in 1901.

In the Leyland Daf Cup Final of 1990 Saunders had a seemingly stonewall penalty denied when referee Vic Callow waved play on after the striker had been flattened by Tranmere 'keeper Eric Nixon. But the Wembley moment that lingers most vividly in the memory is that of Saunders receiving the ball wide on the right and striking a venomous dipper over Nixon's head. Agonisingly, that sensational effort clipped the bar and looped to safety, otherwise the Pirates might have climaxed a fabulous season with a double triumph.

Although Carl left Rovers to play a handful of times for Oxford United and Walsall, he had put down his roots in the Bristol area, and after retiring from professional football he joined Avon and Somerset Police as a community liaison officer dealing with issues of race awareness.

DICK SHEPPARD

1969/70 — 1974/75

DICK SHEPPARD is the man who won the Cup for Bristol Rovers. Okay, so it wasn't *the* Cup, and the final was played at Eastville rather than Wembley, but it would be petty indeed to cavil over such a minor detail.

The piece of silver in question was actually the Watney Cup, being contested in August 1972 by the highest-scoring teams of the previous League campaign who had neither gained promotion nor qualified for Europe, and the Pirates won through to face First Division Sheffield United in the final. When the game ended goalless it was the signal for a penalty shoot-out – and Dick's finest hour.

With Rovers leading 7-6 he dived to his left to smother Ted Hemsley's spot-kick, and ecstatic fans chaired him off the pitch in triumph. It was a sweet moment for the popular Bristolian, who as an asthmatic child had little hope of a career in the game.

Barred by the illness from playing football until the age of 12, Dick recovered to seek his fortune with West Bromwich Albion, and made a promising start at the Hawthorns. He achieved his Division One breakthrough and played in the first League Cup Final to be staged at Wembley, picking up a loser's medal against Queen's Park Rangers, but he never quite became established.

Nevertheless, Dick had garnered precious top-grade experience, and expectations were high when he returned to his home city in June 1969 as one of Fred Ford's last signings as Eastville boss. After a woeful start – he accepted blame for all three goals in a 3-3 draw with Barnsley on his home debut – he justified Fred's faith, emerging as calm, reliable and classy, and an immaculate professional who played a vital part in moulding Bill Dodgin's young team into promotion contenders.

Dick was outstanding in three successive League Cup runs, saving a George Best penalty in a famous victory at Old Trafford in 1972, and was at his peak when disaster struck. He suffered a depressed fracture of the skull in a collision with a Tranmere forward at Prenton Park in January 1973, evoking fearful memories of Bernard Hall's accident six years earlier. Never again was he the same confident performer.

A shaky comeback in a 4-1 Bristol derby defeat nearly two years later was an unfitting footnote to an accomplished tenure between the Pirates' posts. The Watney Cup hero, who became a partner in a local light industrial firm, went on to a spell in Fulham reserves before retiring, his place in Rovers' folklore forever secure. Dick Sheppard died, tragically young, in 1998.

BORN: Bristol, 14.2.45

DIED: Bristol, 18.10.98

ROVERS RECORD:

League: 151 games, 0 goals

FA Cup: 9 games, 0 goals

League Cup: 21 games, 0 goals

Others: 3 games, 0 goals

Total: 184 games, 0 goals

ROVERS HONOURS:

Watney Cup 72/3

OTHER CLUBS:

West Bromwich Albion 65/6-68/9 (39, 0)

Torquay United on loan 73/4 (2, 0)

JAMIE SHORE

1998/99

THE BEST ENGLISH MIDFIELDER since Paul Gascoigne. That's how the coaching staff at the FA Centre of Excellence at Lilleshall rated Jamie Shore's potential when the teenager first joined the England Youth set-up in the early 1990s.

Jamie went on to become part of an England under-16 side that included Emile Heskey, Jamie Carragher and Richard Wright, and the boy from Backwell was fully expected to achieve as much, if not more, than his illustrious team-mates.

At first everything went according to plan as, shortly after his 17th birthday, he became the youngest player ever to sign professional forms for Norwich City. The Canaries, who beat off competition from Manchester United and Liverpool, had been alerted to the boy's exceptional talent by former Rovers chief executive Gordon Bennett, then working at Carrow Road.

But by the time Jamie returned home to Bristol and signed for Ian Holloway in 1998, the 20-year-old had already undergone nine operations on a knee injury sustained just 30 seconds into a Norwich City youth match at Arsenal. It was a problem that was eventually to end Shore's career before the start of the 2002/03 season when, at the age of 24, he told new manager Ray Graydon that he was retiring from football.

In fact, Jamie played just one full term for Rovers, making his first senior appearance as a substitute for Michael Meaker in the home draw against Chesterfield in September 1998 and appearing for the last time in the 3-0 victory over Millwall at The Memorial Stadium in the following April. Fittingly, but overwhelmingly poignantly, he was named man of the match in what was destined to be his farewell outing.

Jamie Shore started just 18 League games for the Pirates, so how can he possibly justify inclusion in this book of Rovers Greats? The answer is simple. Most of those who saw him play would have little hesitation in naming him as one of the most accomplished all-rounders ever to serve the club.

He was a thoroughly modern midfielder and a capable defender, and he could even hold his own as a striker. A combative ball-winner endowed bountifully with both vision and skill, he was able to control a game from his favoured position immediately behind the front-men, and he was both a maker and taker of goals. In virtually every game he played, he was the outstanding player on the pitch.

At Lilleshall, Shore had been coached by some of the most able instructors in the land and it showed in every facet of his game. Yet to his immense credit, he never appeared to be frustrated by playing at a lower level and always gave the impression of loving every minute he was on the pitch.

Arguably his finest performance was in the 5-0 FA Cup defeat of Exeter City at The Memorial Stadium in December 1998, when he scored twice and set up another two goals. After leaving Rovers Jamie set up a soccer academy for promising young players in Bristol.

Born: Backwell, Bristol, 1.9.77

ROVERS RECORD:

League: 18 (6) games, 2 goals

FA Cup: 3 (1) games, 2 goals

Others: 1 game, 1 goal

Total: 22 (7) games, 5 goals

NEIL SLATTER

FROM THE MOMENT Neil Slatter became Bristol Rovers' youngest post-war League footballer, it was obvious that the 16-year-old Welsh full-back was a class above the average callow debutant. His first touch after running on as a substitute for striker Shaun Penny in the April 1981 Eastville encounter with Shrewsbury Town would have done justice to a veteran. The ball came sharply at an awkward height, but Neil chested it down calmly and laid off a perfect pass, thus setting the standard he was to maintain throughout his four campaigns as a Pirate.

He arrived, like so many before him, from Rovers' Cardiff nursery, a slim, shy lad who on first acquaintance seemed hardly likely to flourish in the rough-and-tumble of League football. But when he pulled on his training gear and started to play, his coaches were quick to recognise a potential thoroughbred.

Neil was fast, had a sure touch with both feet and tackled with a power that belied his apparent frailty. Beyond that, the boy had style, a certain assurance on the ball that whispered insistently of a First Division future.

After displaying so much promise on his initial taste of senior action, Neil soon established a regular place, first at left-back but ultimately switching to the right-flank role that became his personal property for three seasons. As he grew in experience his form became more impressive, and it was no surprise when he won his first full cap two days before his 19th birthday.

But such startling progress did not guarantee Neil unanimous approval from the fans. His preference for coolly playing his way out of tight situations at the back, instead of hoofing the ball indiscriminately down the field in time-honoured fashion, led to accusations that he was too casual. In reality, Neil was rarely caught in possession, and his constructive approach – dashing right-wing excursions were a particularly effective tactic – was the springboard for many attacks.

Such flair was hardly likely to go unnoticed, and in the summer of 1985 Neil took his place in the top flight with a £100,000 move to freshly-promoted Oxford United. After that he suffered a chronic reversal of fortune, with his new club returning to the Second Division and a succession of injuries culminating in his premature retirement at the age of 26. As a result the man whose ten appearances for Wales during his Eastville years made him the most capped player in Bristol Rovers' history left the game to work in administration for a supermarket company.

BORN: Cardiff, 30.5.64

ROVERS RECORD:

League: 147 (1) games, 4 goals

FA Cup: 8 games, 1 goal

League Cup: 14 games, 1 goal

Others: 3 games, 0 goals

Total: 172 (1) games, 6 goals

OTHER CLUBS:

Oxford United 85/6-89/90 (91, 6)

Bournemouth on loan 89/90 (6, 0)

22 Wales caps

(10 with Rovers, 12 with Oxford United) 1983-89

BORN: Liverpool, 19.5.54

ROVERS RECORD:

League: 100 (27) games, 40 goals

FA Cup: 8 games, 2 goals

League Cup: 9 (3) games, 3 goals

Others: 2 (1) games, 1 goal

Total: 119 (31) games, 46 goals

OTHER CLUBS:

Middlesbrough 84/5-87/8 (92, 24)

Carlisle United 87/8-88/9 (24, 3)

Darlington 88/9 (10, 4)

ARCHIE STEPHENS

1981/82 — 1984/85

THE MEREST MENTION of the name Archie Stephens to anyone who populated the Eastville terraces in the early to mid-1980s is to invite an immediate response of the staccato chant – 'Ar-chi, Ar-chi, Ar-chi.' It is a spirited salute which will evoke strong memories of the twilight years at the bottom of Muller Road.

Archie Stephens may not have been the most elegant or the most prolific of strikers to have worn the colours of Bristol Rovers, but certainly he was one of the most committed and that counted for a lot as the Pirates faced a perilous future as a team with no ground. The lease at Eastville had expired and the South Stand had burnt down the year before Stephens joined the club, so this was a time for strong characters on and off the pitch.

The blond Merseysider arrived exceptionally late to professional football, being a 27-year-old painter and decorator leading the line for Melksham Town when Terry Cooper signed him on the strength of a 34-goal haul in his only season for the Wiltshiremen. Stephens didn't need to be asked twice whether he'd rather be hanging wallpaper or playing professional football, and he hurled himself at the opportunity with rare vigour.

The big, wiry marksman notched a brace in each of his first two League games, finishing that 1981/82 debut term with 11 strikes, equal to David Williams and only one adrift of top scorer Paul Randall. He wasn't quite as productive in the following campaign but come

Rovers' centenary season of 1983/84, he topped the chart with 13 League goals.

Archie knew exactly how lucky he was to be given the chance to play professional football and he made the most of every minute of his career. In time he achieved cult status with the crowd, even though his game didn't bear particularly deep analysis. His strengths were his physical and mental fortitude, his fitness and his power in the air. It is said that he never pulled out of a challenge in his life and, unquestionably, he scored goals others would have spurned because he was prepared to risk personal injury for the greater good.

Off the pitch Archie was famous for his sharp Scouse wit and warm sense of humour. He was one of the club's most colourful characters and it became something of a tradition during his time at Eastville for Archie to lead the team in a chorus of 'You'll Never Walk Alone' at the end of a players' night out.

Melksham Town had transferred Stephens to Rovers for £3,000 with a 10 per cent sell-on clause, and the money they received when Archie moved to Middlesbrough for £20,000 helped fund new floodlights for the non-League outfit. Archie helped 'Boro rise from the Third Division in 1987 and went on to play League and non-League football in the North before returning briefly to Melksham Town in 1994. In typical style, the battle-hardened 40-year-old marked his second coming with a debut goal against Keynsham Town.

BORN: Bristol, 14.11.46

ROVERS RECORD:

League: 215 (10) games, 11 goals

FA Cup: 9 games, 0 goals

League Cup: 20 games, 1 goal

Others: 6 games, 1 goal

Total: 250 (10) games, 13 goals

ROVERS HONOURS:

Promotion from Third Division 73/4

Watney Cup 72/3

OTHER CLUBS:

West Bromwich Albion 66/7-67/8 (22, 2)

Walsall 68/9-69/70 (7, 0)

Hereford United 77/8-79/80 (60, 2)

KENNY STEPHENS

1970/71 — 1977/78

KENNY STEPHENS was one of the most gifted Bristolians ever to kick a football, yet the man who became an Eastville entertainer of such exciting quality was once agonisingly close to turning his back on the game before he had pulled on a Rovers shirt.

The blond outside-right started his career with West Bromwich Albion and gave some promising First Division performances, but such was the competition at the Hawthorns in the late 1960s that he accepted a move to Walsall. Kenny didn't settle at Fellows Park and, apparently disillusioned with soccer, became a newsagent in the Midlands.

It seemed that a potentially outstanding talent had been lost, but salvation was on hand in the form of Dick Sheppard, a former Albion team-mate who had recently joined the Pirates. He alerted Eastville boss Bill Dodgin who, not one to stand by and let natural ability go to waste, stepped in to offer first a trial and then, in October 1970, a contract.

Kenny grasped the opportunity, and after a period of acclimatisation he proceeded to justify both Dick's hunch and Bill's belief. He dazzled and scored on his Rovers debut at Barnsley, and quickly established himself as a favourite with the home supporters. They revelled in the intricate skills that took him weaving past defenders, gasped at the searing pace that left confused opponents stranded in his wake, and he became a crucially important part of the side which won promotion from the Third Division in 1973/74.

The one aspect of Kenny's game that frustrated was his lack of confidence in front of goal. So often he would create a gilt-edged opening with an inspired dribble, only to squander it with a weak finish or an ill-advised pass. When the strikers were on song this was hardly a disaster, but there were times, especially in the Second Division days of toil, when half a dozen goals from Kenny would have been mightily welcome. In his last four seasons, when he was admittedly adopting more of a midfield role, he failed to find the net at all.

This blemish might have had its roots in the tension he displayed sometimes before a game or, even more markedly, before flying. Twice sent off, he could be a fiery character on the field, although away from the game he was a quiet family man with a mischievous sense of humour. Rovers fans, however, will remember Kenny Stephens for the sheer brilliance with which, without warning, he could illuminate even the dullest game.

BORN: Bristol, 7.11.72

ROVERS RECORD:

League: 137 (34) games, 57 goals

FA Cup: 7 (1) games, 4 goals

League Cup: 11 games, 5 goals

Others: 16 (1) games, 14 goals

Total: 171 (36) games, 80 goals

OTHER CLUBS:

Huddersfield Town 96/7-99/00 (133, 58)

Ipswich Town 99/00-02/03 (75, 27)

Sunderland 02/03- 04/05 (102, 31)

Bristol City 05/06-

MARCUS STEWART

1991/92 — 1995/96

WEMBLEY STADIUM. A warm May afternoon in 1995. There are almost 60,000 fans under the Twin Towers as the Division Two play-off final between Rovers and Huddersfield Town edges into injury time. The Terriers are 2-1 up. Marcus Stewart has already scored one equaliser for Rovers. Now he receives the ball some 40 yards from goal, turns his marker and moves forward. Twenty-five out, Stewart glances up from under his headband, steadies himself and unleashes a howitzer left-foot drive that flies over the outstretched hand of the goalkeeper. Agonisingly, the wonder shot thumps off the crossbar and Marcus Browning is unable to control the rebound, but Stewart's moment of inspiration lives long in the memory.

Marcus occupies a special place in the hearts of Rovers fans not just for his ability but because he is a local lad with an obvious passion for the game. Brought up in the Bristol City hinterland of Hartcliffe, Stewy attracted interest from Nottingham Forest and Southampton before joining Rovers as a trainee. He played his first game aged 18, against Ipswich Town at Twerton Park at the beginning of the 1991/92 season, and became the youngest Pirate to score on his debut since Keith Curle in 1981. In 1994/95 he equalled Dai Ward's record of netting in eight consecutive appearances and the following season became the first Rovers player to score 30 goals in a season since Alfie 'The Baron of Eastville' Biggs in 1963/64.

Yet in his early days Stewart wasn't an automatic first choice. Carl Saunders and John Taylor limited his appearances and his opportunities were further thwarted when manager John Ward employed Taylor as a lone striker. The fans thought Stewart was good enough and he was chosen for England under-21 honours during this perplexing interlude, but obviously Ward felt the young marksman wasn't quite ready.

A combination of Taylor's move to Bradford City for £300,000 in the summer of 1994 and extra practice on the training pitch at Fry's in Keynsham under the tutelage of Dennis Booth gave Stewart his chance alongside Paul Miller or Gareth Taylor. Booth spent hours with Stewart, working on his first touch, and it began to show. Marcus already had pace, vision, and a predatory instinct similar to that of his boyhood hero Gary Lineker, and he was surprisingly effective in the air for a relatively small man. In his final two seasons he combined all of his assets to become one of the most complete centre-forwards to have worn the blue-and-white quarters.

The Rovers board had turned down a £400,000 offer from West Ham for Stewart at the time they had sold John Taylor, but a £1.2 million bid from Huddersfield proved too tempting and the Bristolian moved to the Yorkshire club at the end of the 1995/96 season. If Rovers had owned their ground and if they had achieved promotion Stewart might have stayed, but no true Rovers fan could begrudge the multi-talented marksman his dream of playing in the Premiership, which he did with distinction for Ipswich Town and Sunderland. As for his move to Bristol City in the summer of 2005 ... no comment!

STUART TAYLOR

1965/66 — 1979/80

AFTER STUART TAYLOR'S early, faltering efforts, anyone who predicted that the 6ft 4in centre-half would go on to play more games for Rovers than anyone else in the club's history would have been ridiculed. Fifteen years and more than 600 matches later, the gentle Bristolian could point to the record books and, if he wasn't so modest, claim that he couldn't have been such a bad player after all.

Rarely, if ever, has a single issue split the Eastville following like the Great Stuart Taylor Debate. With the defence going through a shaky period it had been decided that height was the answer, and the gangling 19-year-old was drafted in.

A tidy start in a goalless draw at Workington in April 1966 offered scant indication of the trauma to come. After that encouraging display Stuart often appeared out of his depth against battle-wise Third Division centre-forwards, seemingly diffident about using his strength and aerial power to full advantage.

But still he had his supporters. The pro-Taylor brigade maintained that often he was left exposed in the Rovers rearguard, and that if he was given adequate cover he could come through. His detractors reckoned that he was a major cause of defensive instability, and should go at once.

The most important opinion was that of manager Bert Tann, who stood by his protégé, even when the rest of the world seemed to be against him. Thus did Stuart gain experience and, almost imperceptibly at first, began to improve, so much so that eventually he became one of the most accomplished centre-halves outside the top flight. Supplementing his physical assets with a surprisingly delicate touch on the ball, he played some of his most constructive football in 1968/69, when Larry Lloyd's dominance at the back allowed him to move forward.

Often Stuart, an integral part of the 1973/74 promotion line-up, was the subject of transfer speculation. Indeed, he was checked out by most of the country's leading clubs, but they all found him 'too nice'. When Rovers gave their former skipper a free transfer in May 1980 he could have gone to Chelsea, but he chose instead to manage Bath City before reverting to his trade as a plumber.

There are those who will always say of Stuart Taylor that if he'd had half the 'devil' of Larry Lloyd he'd have reached the First Division and played for England. Perhaps so, but back at Eastville his boots would have taken an awful lot of filling.

BORN: Bristol, 18.4.47

ROVERS RECORD:

League: 546 games, 28 goals

FA Cup: 38 games, 3 goals

League Cup: 36 games, 3 goals

Others: 7 games, 0 goals

Total: 627 games, 34 goals

ROVERS HONOURS:

Promotion from Division Three 73/4

Watney Cup 72/3

MARTIN THOMAS

1976/77 — 1981/82

THERE WAS A TIME when Martin Thomas seemed set for an illustrious international future. He had established second place in the pecking order of Welsh goalkeepers, even being rated above the young Neville Southall, and as the 1980s dawned only Wrexham's experienced Dai Davies stood between the accomplished Rovers rookie and the job of guarding his country's net. Sadly, the lucky breaks every young sportsman needs to reach the top were never to be his.

Martin, who hailed from a rugby-mad mining community where it was practically an act of heresy to play the 'soft' game of soccer, had all the necessary attributes to make the grade. A strapping six-footer and a fitness fanatic, he was agile, strong and blessed with prehensile handling powers that made him equally adept at taking shots on his line or crosses near the edge of the penalty box.

But the most striking of Martin's exemplary qualifications was an unflappable temperament that from his earliest days at Eastville saw him emerge unscathed from many a daunting situation. As a 15-year-old he was beaten six times in a reserve game, yet he walked off the pitch at the end as man of the match, a feat of level-headedness matched by the way he handled his debut against Charlton at The Valley in January 1977. By then 17, he made an elementary error to concede an early goal, yet he went on to show the sort of form that was soon to win him the first-team berth at Jim Eadie's expense.

There followed three-and-a-half seasons of splendid performances as a Second Division regular before his progress was painfully interrupted by a dislocated finger that demanded an operation. Martin was sidelined for the rest of 1980/81, which ended in Rovers' relegation, and on his return he was hampered by residual stiffness in the joint. Though his form was acceptable, he had perhaps lost a slight edge and was unable to dislodge his replacement, Phil Kite, from the side.

By now rivals were also leapfrogging Martin in the queue for the Welsh jersey and, after turning down Tottenham Hotspur, he opted for a fresh start at Newcastle. He was only 24, no age for a 'keeper, and there was still ample time to fulfil his potential. But, despite winning that long-awaited cap while at St James' Park, more injuries led to frustration and a move to Birmingham, where Martin continued to be a capable custodian instead of the outstanding one he had once seemed destined to be.

BORN: Senghenydd, Glamorgan,
28.11.59

ROVERS RECORD:

League: 162 games, 0 goals

FA Cup: 9 games, 0 goals

League Cup: 13 games, 0 goals

Others: 4 games, 0 goals

Total: 188 games, 0 goals

OTHER CLUBS:

Cardiff City on loan 82/3 (15, 0)

Southend United on loan 82/3 (6, 0)

Newcastle United 82/3-87/8 (118, 0)

Middlesbrough on loan 84/5 (4, 0)

Birmingham City 88/9-92/3 (144, 0)

1 Wales cap (won with Newcastle United)
1986

BORN: Huntingdon, 30.6.66

ROVERS RECORD:

League: 250 (3) games, 11 goals

FA Cup: 11 games, 0 goals

League Cup: 16 games, 1 goal

Others: 19 (1) games, 2 goals

Total: 296 (4) games, 14 goals

OTHER CLUBS:

Grimsby Town 88/9-90/1 (105, 5)

Queen's Park Rangers 90/1-91/2 (29, 2)

Grimsby Town on loan 92/3 (4, 0)

Walsall 00/01-01/02 (51, 2)

Rushden and Diamonds 01/02-02/03 (19, 0)

ANDY TILLSON

1992/93 — 1999/2000

THOSE PLAYERS WHO KNOW Andy Tillson well, either as team-mates or opponents, are unanimous in their assessment of him as one of the finest professionals of his generation. The 6ft 2in central defender lacked a yard of pace, but he compensated for that by leadership qualities that made him an exemplary club captain.

Tillson's arrival in Bristol was a peculiar affair. It was the club directors, rather than manager Dennis Rofe, who signed him on the recommendation of QPR boss Gerry Francis in November 1992 for a club record fee of £370,000. Andy's first game for Rovers was to be Rofe's last, a 5-1 mauling away to Wolves, after which the manager was replaced by Malcolm Allison – already at the club as a consultant – who lasted for just four months as his 'whirl' formation sent Rovers spiralling towards relegation from Division One.

Thus Tillson played for Rofe, Allison, caretaker boss Steve Cross and Allison's successor John Ward in his first five months at Rovers, while operating in a rearguard that was nearing the end of its time with the impending departures of Geoff Twentyman, Ian Alexander and Steve Yates. There was also the small matter of demotion in his first season with Rovers, who finished eight points adrift at the bottom of Division One with a shocking goal difference of minus 32. It must have taken all of the newcomer's immense courage and self-belief to build so impressive a Rovers career after such a perilous start.

Andy formed a decent central-defensive partnership with Billy Clark, first under John Ward and then Ian Holloway, but excelled in his subsequent stalwart combination with Steve Foster and Andy Thomson which was the foundation of the new manager's promotion hopes. Tillson organised the defence magnificently, making sure that the simple things were always done well and leading the team by example. He took seriously his responsibilities as club captain and was instrumental in helping younger players graduate into the first team. The fans warmed to Tillson because they knew he was playing to his full potential and had the ability to perform in a higher division, perhaps even in the Premier League. As long as Tillson was in place, the side seemed in safe hands, in much the same way as when Stuart Taylor marshalled the back line in the 1970s.

When Holloway's team was dismantled after failure to reach the 1999/00 play-offs, most fans expected Cureton and Roberts to move on, but the sale of Andy Tillson to Ray Graydon's Walsall for a reported £10,000 (later it was revealed to be a free transfer) seemed inexplicable. In his first season Tillson captained Walsall to promotion to Division One while Rovers were relegated to Division Three.

Andy, who had kept his home in Bath, eventually returned to the West Country as a player/coach with Team Bath alongside former Rovers goalkeeper Brian Parkin. There are many fans who would welcome him back to Rovers as coach or even manager.

BORN: Liverpool, 10.3.59.

ROVERS RECORD:

League: 248 (4) games, 6 goals

FA Cup: 13 (1) games, 0 goals

League Cup: 13 games, 1 goal

Others: 19 games, 0 goals

Total: 293 (5) games, 7 goals

ROVERS HONOURS:

Third Division Championship 89/90

Leyland Daf Cup Finalist 89/90

OTHER CLUBS:

Preston North End 83/4-85/6 (98, 4)

GEOFF TWENTYMAN

1986/87 — 1992/93

GERRY FRANCIS may have been the man who assembled the team known as 'Ragbag Rovers' but on the pitch it was Geoff Twentyman and fellow defender Vaughan Jones who put the Francis masterplan into practice. Such was the influence of the pair in the epoch-making 1989/90 campaign – when the Pirates lifted the Third Division crown and appeared in the Leyland Daf Cup Final at Wembley – that they were widely expected to return to the club in managerial roles following the dismissal of Dennis Rofe in 1992. Instead, Malcolm Allison was appointed, and although Geoff did later become assistant boss under Ian Holloway, eventually he chose a path outside the game as a sports journalist with BBC Radio Bristol.

As a schoolboy, Twentyman had been on the books at Anfield, where his father – also Geoff – had been a stalwart defensive wing-half during the 1950s before becoming Liverpool's chief scout. But Geoff Jnr didn't make the senior grade with the Reds and he had dropped into non-League football with Chorley Town, while studying for a banking career, when he was given a chance to turn professional with Preston North End in 1983.

Three seasons later Twerton Park chief Bobby Gould took Twentyman from Deepdale and the 27-year-old swiftly established himself as a consistent performer at the rearguard's core. But it was under Francis that the big Merseysider flourished most impressively, forming an efficient partnership with Steve Yates, the former's experience complemented ideally by the latter's pace.

Twentyman was club captain during Rovers' rise from the Third Division to the Second and he played in 162 consecutive League games over three campaigns, a sequence broken in unusual fashion at the end of 1988/89. Geoff's brother had asked him to be his best man, but the wedding date fell shortly before a play-off clash with Fulham. Francis banned Twentyman from attending the ceremony, but the skipper put family before football, travelled against his manager's wishes and was dropped from the play-offs. At this point he feared for his Rovers career, but Francis reinstated him at the beginning of 1989/90 and the stopper was ever-present throughout that unforgettable term.

The Pirates were unbeaten at home for the first time in their history and lost only five of their 46 League games, such was the strength of a back four comprising Ian Alexander, Yates, Twentyman and Jones. The ecstasy at Twerton Park when promotion was clinched by a 3-0 defeat of Bristol City, followed by the carnival high-jinks at Blackpool when 5,000 Rovers fans witnessed the claiming of the title, marked the high point of Twentyman's Rovers tenure.

However, he was no fair-weather footballer, having proved his commitment to the cause during the difficult early years at Twerton when the club teetered on the brink of oblivion. It was thanks to the character and leadership of players such as Geoff Twentyman that Rovers not only survived, but went on to taste Championship glory.

BORN: Birmingham, 2.6.64

ROVERS RECORD:

League: 46 (36) games, 13 goals

FA Cup: 0 (5) games, 1 goal

League Cup: 0 (5) games, 0 goals

Others: 0 (4) games, 0 goals

Total: 46 (50) games, 14 goals

OTHER CLUBS:

Aston Villa 81/2-87/8 (181, 39)

Rangers 87/8-90/1 (106, 32)

Liverpool 91/2-94/5 (94, 14)

Stoke City on loan 93/4 (9, 2)

Wolverhampton Wanderers on loan 94/5 (11, 3)

Southampton 95/6 (5, 0)

Swindon Town 96/7-99/00 (112, 25)

1 England cap (won with Rangers) 1991

MARK WALTERS

1999/2000 — 2001/02

IN THE TROUBLED DAYS following the departure of manager Ian Holloway to Queen's Park Rangers, the sight of former England international Mark Walters surging down the left wing, performing his trademark step-over or placing the ball for a curling free-kick into the box, provided rare comfort for Rovers fans.

Walters was in the twilight of his career when he joined Rovers from Swindon Town in November 1999, his goal-scoring record was far from remarkable and the knee injuries sustained from a lifetime of battles with full-backs meant that sometimes he would not last the full 90 minutes. But in terms of skill, application and teamwork, Wally will long be remembered as being a credit to the club and for giving Gasheads a glimpse of the class that saw him achieve plenty at the highest level.

It was Ian Holloway's commitment to playing a passing game and his belief in wingers that tempted the England international to join Rovers. Whether he played as a traditional wingman in a 4-4-2 formation or as a wing-back in a 3-5-2 role, Walters immediately gave balance to the team and his attitude was top-notch. Still he was able to show flashes of the flair of old, while his discipline made up for an inevitable decline in pace. If he couldn't beat his man or whip in a cross, invariably Mark would earn a throw-in or corner.

Walters joined a seasoned midfield unit of David Hillier, Ronnie Mauge and Vitalijs Astafjevs. With great things expected of youngsters Simon Bryant and Lewis Hogg, a solid defence built around Andy Tillson, Steve Foster and Andy Thomson and an abundance of riches up front in Jamie Cureton and Jason Roberts, plus youngsters Nathan Ellington and Bobby Zamora on the rise, Mark Walters was exactly the sort of experienced player who might have helped steer Rovers to promotion.

In his key role he did everything that was asked of him (and more), but when Rovers missed out on the play-offs in 1999/2000, Holloway was forced to dispose of crucial players, then left the Memorial Stadium himself midway through the devastating relegation season of 2000/01. Thus marooned in an unenviable situation, Walters fought as hard as any other player in the subsequent relegation battle which was doomed to failure as the club embarked upon the darkest days in its history.

Walters stuck with Rovers in their first season in the bottom division as Gerry Francis returned to the club. There was hope among fans that if the Midlander took on a coaching role alongside Francis, the pair could bring through several promising youngsters and swiftly guide Rovers to promotion.

But Francis left on Christmas Eve and Rovers suffered another season of abject despair, at the end of which Walters departed to join non-League Ilkeston Town. In the circumstances, it could only be viewed as an honourable exit. It had always been a pleasure, and often a privilege, to watch Mark Walters play football, even though there was little else to cheer Rovers fans during his time at the club.

ALAN WARBOYS

1972/73 — 1976/77

HOW EASTVILLE LOVED its folk heroes. Since the war there had been Bamford and Bradford, Biggs and Jarman, and when Alan Warboys came along it was soon obvious that he was the latest in that illustrious line. It was partly to do with ability, perhaps more with personality, but a player either had that certain something, or he hadn't. Big Alan, most emphatically, had it.

The powerful, ever-hustling centre-forward was not quite 24 when Don Megson signed him for a Rovers record of £35,000 from Sheffield United in March 1973, yet already he had sampled life in all four flights of the Football League. He signalled his intentions with promising form in the few weeks remaining of that campaign, before catapulting to national prominence with a goal glut in the early part of the following season.

Alan and nippy fellow Yorkshireman Bruce Bannister struck up a potent partnership, the little man benefiting hugely from the newcomer's marauding presence, and they were dubbed 'Smash and Grab' as Rovers took a seven-point lead at the top of the Third Division. The highlight of this heady interlude, savoured by millions on TV, was the 8-2 annihilation of Brighton at the Goldstone Ground. That day

Alan scored four and laid on three; but for an eye injury which prevented him adding to his tally, he might have reduced the already livid Seagulls' boss Brian Clough to apoplexy.

The Pirates' dynamic six-footer was emerging as a fine footballer, his nickname 'Smash' doing him less than justice. Admittedly he did have many of the virtues of a battering ram, both in the air and on the ground, and the fans adored his habit of thumping shots at goal with either foot from anything up to 30 yards. But also he was capable of smooth control and slick, even intricate, passing movements.

Warboys' value to the side was proved when he was absent for a long spell in the New Year with a strained hamstring and results fell off; promotion was still attained, but the title slipped away. In the Second Division, with the team often under defensive pressure, opportunities and goals were harder to come by, but easy-going Alan completed four happy years at Eastville before a rift with Megson precipitated a £30,000 switch to Fulham. Later as a publican in Yorkshire, he retained a genuine warmth for Rovers and their supporters. The feeling, he'd be glad to know, was entirely mutual.

BORN: Goldthorpe, Yorkshire, 14.4.49

ROVERS RECORD:

League: 141 (3) games, 53 goals

FA Cup: 8 games, 4 goals

League Cup: 10 games, 3 goals

Others: 2 games, 0 goals

Total: 161 (3) games, 60 goals

ROVERS HONOURS:

Promotion from Third Division 73/4

OTHER CLUBS:

Sheffield Wednesday 68/9-70/1 (71, 13)

Cardiff City 70/1-72/3 (60, 27)

Sheffield United 72/3 (7, 0)

Fulham 76/7-77/8 (19, 2)

Hull City 77/8-78/9 (49, 9)

Doncaster Rovers 79/80-81/2 (89, 21)

BORN: Barry, Glamorgan, 16.7.34

DIED: Cambridge, 12.1.96

ROVERS RECORD:

League: 175 games, 90 goals

FA Cup: 13 games, 6 goals

League Cup: 1 game, 0 goals

Total: 189 games, 96 goals

OTHER CLUBS:

Cardiff City 60/1-61/2 (35, 18)

Watford 62/3-63/4 (59, 31)

Brentford 63/4-64/5 (47, 11)

2 Wales caps (1 won with Rovers, 1 with Cardiff City)

1958-61

DAI WARD

1954/55 — 1960/61

A GOAL SPREE BY DAI WARD took Bristol Rovers closer to the top division than at any other time in their history. The supremely confident – some might say cocky – young Welshman was called up in the spring of 1956 to deputise for the injured Geoff Bradford. He responded by scoring nine times in eight outings and, if the Pirates had won their last two games instead of losing to Leeds United and Liverpool, they would have reached the premier flight.

Dai was a born opportunist, an inside-forward of pace, skill and bravery whose natural habitat was the penalty box. He preyed mercilessly on scraps from the table of Bradford and Alfie Biggs, was ever alert for rebounds from Peter Hooper piledrivers, and also had the talent to fashion his own chances, the overhead kick being a particularly pleasing party trick.

Ward was seen at his sharpest against Doncaster Rovers on one damp, misty Saturday afternoon shortly before Christmas 1956. In that mid-table encounter – the memory of which clothes Eastville in a cosy romantic glow, though at the time it probably seemed like any other foot-stamping winter's day – Dai lashed a four-minute hat-trick past Harry Gregg, later to star for Manchester United and Northern Ireland.

The boy from Barry continued to demonstrate his potential and in November 1958, in the season in which he topped the Rovers scoring charts with 27 goals in 38 matches, he won a richly deserved first Welsh cap. An injury to Dave Bowen prompted a late reshuffle in which Dai was switched to left-half and, though he created a goal for Ivor Allchurch, he failed to do himself justice and lost his place.

Meanwhile, relations with Rovers boss Bert Tann, who was not endeared by the player's argumentative streak, were often what newspapers like to describe as stormy, and eventually Dai embarked on a bitter battle to leave the club, which he criticised for lack of ambition. At one time he threatened to quit the game, and actually took a job as an ice-cream salesman. The unhappy saga ended with his transfer to First Division Cardiff City in February 1961.

Predictably, he scored regularly at the higher level, and won a second cap. But he fell out of favour at Ninian Park, too, and saw out his playing days with Watford and Brentford, an anti-climactic finale to a career that should have hit the heights.

RAY WARREN

1935/36 — 1955/56

RAY WARREN was the spirit of Bristol Rovers incarnate. Nowhere has a passion for the Pirates burned more intensely than in the staunch heart of this sandy-haired, deceptively spare Bristolian who performed heroics at the centre of defence, at first in seasons of grave adversity and then in days of heady triumph. He is remembered today as the greatest captain the club ever had.

On Ray's retirement Bert Tann, Rovers' most eloquent and formidable manager of modern times, began an exhaustive search for a comparable lieutenant to carry his soccer creed on to the field. Privately, Bert believed he was attempting the impossible, and so it was to prove.

Ray made his debut before the war as an inside-right, but as the side struggled in the nether reaches of the Third Division South it was wisely decided to employ his combative qualities at centre-half. In 1939 soccer took a back seat, but Ray played a leading part in wartime competitions, turning out for his own club and also guesting for Leeds United, Bristol City and Bath City.

By 1946 he was at his peak and ready to lead the Rovers, rarely far from the foot of the table, through a series of stirring rearguard actions.

Ray was an inspiration, always to be found where the battle was at its fiercest, roaring his instructions and brooking no arguments. Despite his comparative lack of stature for a stopper – even with his boots on he was an inch short of six feet – he was not often bested in the air, even when pitted against the likes of Tommy Lawton and Trevor Ford. Meanwhile, if his methods on the deck were not exactly scientific, they were undeniably effective.

Happily, there were less frenetic times ahead. As Bert Tann's influence grew the team improved, and in 1953 they finished top of the Third Division South. Ray played a vital part, not only through his football but also by communicating the new boss's demands – so different from those of the previous manager, Brough Fletcher – to his colleagues.

In the Second Division, although by now 35, he blossomed as a player, adopting a more constructive approach without losing the aggression that was integral to his game. Ray took a pub after eventually departing from Eastville, and died in 1988. He left a legacy of memories that will survive as long as the name of Bristol Rovers itself.

BORN: Bristol, 23.6.18

DIED: Bristol, 13.3.88

ROVERS RECORD:

League: 450 games, 28 goals

FA Cup: 36 games, 1 goal

Total: 486 games, 29 goals

ROVERS HONOURS:

Third Division South Championship 52/3

BORN: Bristol, 11.5.25

ROVERS RECORD:

League: 323 games, 19 goals

FA Cup: 29 games, 2 goals

League Cup: 2 games, 0 goals

Total: 354 games, 21 goals

JOHN 'JOSSER' WATLING

1947/48 — 1961/62

HAD THERE BEEN TREES AT EASTVILLE, then 'Josser' Watling would have charmed the birds off them. He was the court jester with the sweet left foot, the man who christened Alfie Biggs 'The Baron', got Bill Roost off a booking by telling the referee that the outspoken inside-forward was deaf, and successfully switched from winger to full-back without the remotest reduction in his entertainment value.

Of course, 'Josser' could play a bit, too. He joined Rovers on leaving the Navy in 1945, and three years later he made his League debut in the number-11 shirt. For the next four seasons the left-wing berth was usually his, the only major interruptions being short spells when George Petherbridge switched flanks, and a period when Soundwell boy Brian Bush came into contention.

Watling established himself as a trickster who, in the words of a team-mate, put his foot on the ball and shook his backside. On gaining possession, he would dribble with tantalising deliberation towards his full-back, thus inviting all manner of rash challenges, and then whisk the ball away at the last possible moment. Having beaten his man, 'Josser' would reveal another speciality, the long cross that seemed to hang in the air as it floated towards the predatory heads of Geoff Bradford and Vic Lambden.

Offsetting his talent on the ball, however, was a lack of pace and a dearth of goal-scoring power that at times induced manager Bert Tann to drop him. Thus it was that the winger missed out on a Third Division South Championship medal in 1952/53, though he was recalled for the final four matches to help revive Rovers' faltering impetus.

In the next season, he prospered in the higher grade until the arrival of Peter Hooper cast doubts over his future. Two years of frustration ensued until Bert had a brainwave and converted 'Josser' into a constructive left-back. It was a classic case of poacher-turned-gamekeeper, with the former flankman being well tuned to the ruses employed by wily wingers. Even Blackburn's brilliant Bryan Douglas, rampant against most defenders and only weeks away from winning his first cap, was mastered.

'Josser' Watling went on to become club captain and enjoy four seasons in his new role before retiring, later returning to Eastville as a coach and scout. Thus was a new generation introduced to one of football's natural comedians and most priceless characters.

DEVON WHITE

1987/88 — 1991/92

IF GERRY FRANCIS was an unlikely fairy god-mother, then what price Devon White as Cinderella? But in the story of the towering striker's recruitment to Twerton Park, there is no doubting the roles played by the Bristol Rovers boss and the Lincoln City reject who had given up professional football to become an electrician.

During his own brief playing stint as a Pirate, Francis had encountered Devon as a clumsy yet chaos-inducing substitute, and he had marvelled at the time that the 6ft 3in front-man was not a first-team regular. Two years later, with Rovers in need of cover for Robbie Turner, Gerry fell to wondering what had become of the gangling youngster with so much raw potential. After enterprising detective work, White was located at his new job and, on getting over the shock of a message from the former England captain, he accepted first a trial and then a two-year contract.

Soon, before he'd had time to pinch himself, the muscular Midlander was off on the next stage of his incredible journey. Turner was delayed in traffic on the way to Rovers' home clash with Aldershot in August 1987 and Devon was drafted in. He scored that day, and in the next match, and in the one after that; henceforth, not surprisingly, he was beloved of the fans. The blue-and-white army relished chanting his nickname 'Bru-no, Bru-no', in tribute to his supposed likeness to the boxer Frank, but opposing centre-halves did not share their affection.

For them, Devon was one of the most awkward propositions in the League. Lumbering along, arms and legs flailing, he created a space around himself on which it was neither easy nor comfortable to encroach. Though he scored his quota of goals – the brace that shattered Bristol City on that never-to-be-forgotten night at Twerton Park when the Pirates clinched promotion to the Second Division took pride of place for pure value – he was most effective as a provider.

His striking partners, most notably Gary Penrice, benefited hugely from the nicks and rebounds that tended to ensue when the big man got the ball. In the early days Devon's control was, shall we say, rudimentary, but he strove unceasingly, and with marked success, to improve it.

Often the treatment of such an honest player by referees seemed harsh, for the fouls he sometimes committed invariably stemmed from ungainliness rather than malice.

After being so instrumental in securing promotion, Devon White's forceful presence was felt during Rovers' first two campaigns in the higher flight before he embarked on a six-club odyssey over the next seven years. Everywhere he went, hard-pressed opponents could be excused for cursing Gerry Francis's memory – or should that be his magic wand?

BORN: Nottingham, 2.3.64

ROVERS RECORD:

League: 190 (12) games, 53 goals

FA Cup: 10 games, 3 goals

League Cup: 9 games, 2 goals

Others: 19 games, 2 goals

Total: 228 (12) games, 60 goals

ROVERS HONOURS:

Third Division Championship 89/90

Leyland Daf Cup Finalist 89/90

OTHER CLUBS:

Lincoln City 84/5-85/6 (29, 4)

Cambridge United 91/2-92/3 (22, 4)

Queen's Park Rangers 92/3-94/5 (26, 9)

Notts County 94/5-95/6 (40, 15)

Watford 95/6-96/7 (38, 7)

Notts County 96/7-97/8 (15, 2)

Shrewsbury Town 97/8-98/9 (43, 10)

BORN: Chipping Sodbury, Glos, 2.1.59

ROVERS RECORD:

League: 135 (16) games, 44 goals

FA Cup: 10 (1) games, 5 goals

League Cup: 10 games, 3 goals

Others: 5 (2) games, 1 goal

Total: 160 (19) games, 53 goals

OTHER CLUBS:

Luton Town 79/80-81/2 (72, 25)

Charlton Athletic 82/3 (29, 12)

Lincoln City on loan 82/3 (3, 0)

Luton Town on loan 82/3 (4, 0)

Swindon Town 86/7-93/4 (244, 83)

Hereford United 94/5-95/6 (76, 44)

Cardiff City 96/7-97/8 (67, 15)

STEVE WHITE

1977/78 — 1979/80 & 1983/84 — 1985/86

STEVE WHITE was the man who replaced the local hero, and he was never allowed to forget it. The decision to sell charismatic goal-scorer Paul Randall to Stoke City in December 1978 was taken by the Rovers board, but that did not stop a strident section of the Eastville crowd from regularly venting its spleen on the hard-working, skilful but less flamboyant performer who took over the terrace darling's front-line role.

It amounted to spiteful, illogical abuse of a dedicated professional who, while lacking Paul's lethal finishing prowess, was by far the more balanced all-round player. In contrast to his predecessor, who relied so much on instinct, Steve was a thinking footballer, a strong-running, somewhat awkward-looking striker who would toil selflessly to set up chances for colleagues as well as score his own quota of goals.

He was a man who might find the net from a difficult angle and then fluff a comparative sitter, but even when the tide of a game was flowing against him he would never shirk his responsibilities, always remaining eager for the ball. If anything Steve, an enthusiastic trainer and a perfectionist who was his own sternest critic, appeared to thrive on adversity, often answering his barrackers with a particularly effective display.

The White cocktail of grit and goal power – he netted 20 times in 46 starts, a highly creditable ratio, during his first spell with Rovers –

certainly impressed Luton Town, who signed him for £195,000 in December 1979. His Second Division travels took him to Charlton before newly appointed Pirates boss David Williams brought him home for £35,000 in August 1983.

This time, ironically, one of Steve's striking partners was Paul Randall, the innocent cause of so much discomfiture, and much was expected from what seemed to be a pairing of complementary talents. In fact, they proved a disappointing combination with which neither David nor his successor, Bobby Gould, persevered.

In general, White's second Eastville stint, during which he turned out occasionally in midfield, was a success, and he continued to show his worth in a stalwart eight-season sojourn at Swindon after moving to the County Ground in 1986, especially during the tactically enlightened regime of Ossie Ardiles.

Steve, who later served Hereford United and Cardiff City and was still playing League football in his 40th year, proved conclusively that he was an accomplished performer, at least to the level of the old Second Division. What a shame that a scandal over illegal payments at Swindon – a shambles in which he was not personally implicated – scotched his chance of testing his talents in the top flight, the League punishing the Wiltshiremen by denying them their hard-won promotion in 1990.

DAVID WILLIAMS

1975/76 — 1984/85

DAVID WILLIAMS was perhaps the most cultured midfielder Bristol Rovers ever had, yet there is a lingering suspicion, fuelled by achievements with Norwich City and Wales at the end of his playing career, that throughout his Eastville prime his vast potential was barely being tapped.

Not that David didn't throw his all into six seasons of scrapping to avoid the drop into the Third Division and four more of striving to climb back out. But it was hard not to feel that such a masterful exponent of the passing game, both long and short, should have been parading his talents at Old Trafford and Anfield, Highbury and White Hart Lane, rather than some of soccer's more humble outposts.

David was never the all-action, firecracker type; his were skills to sit back and savour. He appeared to stroll, now changing the angle of attack with a raking cross-field drive, then freeing his winger with a penetrating pass through a posse of opponents. Calm and constructive amid the utmost chaos, he boasted assured ball control that afforded him time and space to review his options, a crucial creative asset.

At various times David was employed in central defence, at full-back and even up front, but the middle of the field, where his prompting abilities were supplemented by a precious penchant for blasting long-range goals – he averaged ten per season in the late 1970s – was unquestionably his most effective position.

The switches were useful, however, in offering fresh challenges for an intelligent man who as a young teacher had initially been reluctant to forsake the classroom for fear of getting bored, and had consequently played as a part-timer.

The drawbacks to David's game were generally reckoned to be a lack of pace, for which he compensated by quickness of thought, and a shortage of aggression. But his approach acquired added bite when he became player-manager in 1983, a role in which he showed much enterprise to keep Rovers in successive Third Division promotion races.

He was 30 when he took his talents to classier realms, joining Norwich City for £40,000 in the summer of 1985, and he helped the Canaries reach the top flight in his first season.

David excelled among the elite and went on to win five caps before becoming assistant manager at Carrow Road, where his influence on an attractive team was clearly immense. Had he moved earlier he might have scaled the heights, but Bristol Rovers would have been immeasurably the poorer.

BORN: Cardiff, 11.3.55

ROVERS RECORD:

League: 342 (10) games, 66 goals

FA Cup: 18 (1) games, 7 goals

League Cup: 30 games, 6 goals

Others: 12 games, 2 goals

Total: 402 (11) games, 81 goals

OTHER CLUBS:

Norwich City 85/6-87/8 (60, 11)

Bournemouth 92/3 (1, 0)

5 Wales caps (won with Norwich City) 1986

MANAGER:

Bristol Rovers 1983-85

Wales (as caretaker) 1988

GERAINT WILLIAMS

WHEN ROVERS PLAYER-MANAGER David Williams told his midfield namesake Geraint 'You do my running and tackling for me and I'll score the goals,' there was probably an element of jest in the statement. But Williams the younger took the sentiment seriously and went on to base a long and distinguished career on the selfless attributes of bravery, fitness and no small amount of skill.

Geraint was one of the many products of Stan Montgomery's famous Welsh nursery, which he joined as an 11-year-old. He was recruited as an Eastville apprentice when Bobby Campbell was boss and was nurtured by Harold Jarman in the youth team before being given his chance at senior level by Terry Cooper. Williams made his debut at home against Sheffield Wednesday in a side that included Cooper, Gary Mabbutt, David Williams, Phil Bater and Mike Barrett, who scored his first League goal in the 3-3 draw.

At this time Rovers had an excellent reputation for bringing through their own youngsters, who were encouraged to play an attractive, attacking game. Sadly, these values weren't enough to keep Rovers in the Second Division and they were relegated in 1981 (along with Bristol City), finishing the season bottom of the table 13 points adrift of safety. Off the pitch the situation was no better as the Pirates felt the effects of the disastrous sale of Eastville in 1940. The lease on the ground had run out and the series of events was under way that would lead to Rovers' departure for Twerton Park in 1986. The situation became even worse when a mystery fire destroyed Eastville's South Stand at the beginning of 1980/81.

It was thanks to players of the character of Geraint Williams that the club survived such difficult times. Following Terry Cooper's surprising dismissal in October 1981, Bobby Gould took over as manager and the young Williams continued to grow in stature. But it was when David Williams replaced Gould to become the youngest League manager at the beginning of 1983/84 that Geraint enjoyed his greatest influence. Although this team never fully flourished, it will be fondly remembered as an elegant, brave footballing side, with Geraint Williams the midfield engine. There was a remarkable bond between the players and fans – nicknamed the Famous Five Thousand – at this point in Rovers' history, a sense of everyone pulling together in the face of an uncertain future.

Undoubtedly Geraint thought his future lay with the club and he bought a new house in Downend in 1985. But even as he waited for new carpets to be delivered, David Williams arrived to tell him that the Rovers board had accepted a £40,000 offer from Derby County. Geraint played more than 300 games for the Rams before becoming a record signing and playing in the Premiership with Ipswich Town. He won 13 full international caps for Wales and saw out his League playing days in 1999 with Colchester United, whom he went on to serve as assistant manager.

Born: Treorchy, Glamorgan, 5.1.62

ROVERS RECORD:

League: 138 (3) games, 8 goals

FA Cup: 9 (1) games, 2 goals

League Cup: 13 games, 0 goals

Others: 5 games, 0 goals

Total: 165 (4) games, 10 goals

OTHER CLUBS

Derby County 84/5-91/2 (277, 9)

Ipswich Town 92/3-97/8 (217, 3)

Colchester United 98/9 (39, 0)

13 Wales caps 1987-95

STEVE YATES

1986/87 — 1993/94

IT WAS A TRYING AFTERNOON for Luther Blissett. The fleet-footed Watford and former AC Milan striker was several years past his England prime, but still a considerable handful, when he faced Bristol Rovers' promising teenage defender Steve Yates in a reserve encounter at Forest Green.

That day at the Cotswolds hillside home of the Pirates' second string, Luther, an honest individual who never gave less than maximum effort, was hardly allowed to put boot to ball. Steve more than matched him for pace and perpetually blocked his route to goal in a storming performance that confirmed the blond Bristolian's enormous potential.

But neither that excellent showing nor his subsequent progress to become a vital part of Gerry Francis's 1989/90 Third Division Championship side surprised anyone who had known Yates since his schooldays. He seemed to want nothing out of life but to play football. A perfectionist who was rarely satisfied with his own displays, he toiled endlessly to improve his skills and fitness, and was ever eager to learn.

Allied to dedication and speed was a talent for reading the game, often anticipating danger before it materialised, that made him a natural for the centre of defence. Here, clearly, was a golden prospect, yet when it was time for Steve to turn professional the club almost lost him. Funds were so short that Rovers couldn't afford his wages and, had not fans in the Presidents Club come up with the cash, he would have been released.

Having impressed on his senior debut, as a 17-year-old at Darlington in March 1987, Steve played in the following game, after which he waited 18 months for his next and decisive opportunity. He stepped in for the injured Billy Clark in the autumn of 1988, and quickly it became apparent that he was there to stay.

Though improvement was needed in his passing and aerial work, he was rarely beaten to the ball, and once in possession he refused to take the slightest risk. He showed a priceless instinct in the timing of tackles, knowing when to hold off and when to commit himself, and proved an ideal foil for the taller Geoff Twentyman, an able but more ponderous performer.

Still a mere 20 years old when Rovers rose to the second flight, Yates appeared to be on the threshold of a glittering career. It was a juncture at which he might have been whisked away to the game's higher echelons, but he remained at the club for three more seasons before following Gerry Francis to Queen's Park Rangers, at a cost of £750,000, in August 1993.

The West Countryman took a season to settle in London, but gradually he revealed his class, proving himself capable of performing in the Premiership yet without quite blossoming in the expansive manner expected by plenty of shrewd observers.

After dropping out of the top flight with Rangers in 1996, he remained at Loftus Road for three more terms before moving to Tranmere, and in 2004/05 he was voted players' player of the year at Huddersfield.

BORN: Bristol, 29.1.70

ROVERS RECORD:

League: 196 (1) games, 0 goals

FA Cup: 11 games, 0 goals

League Cup: 9 games, 0 goals

Others: 21 games, 0 goals

Total: 237 (1) games, 0 goals

ROVERS HONOURS:

Third Division Championship 89/90

Leyland Daf Cup Finalist 89/90

OTHER CLUBS:

Queen's Park Rangers 93/4-98/9 (134, 2)

Tranmere Rovers 99/00-01/02 (113, 7)

Sheffield United 02/03 (12, 0)

Huddersfield Town 03/04- (52,1)

JUNIOR AGOGO
2003/04 –
71 (19) games, 27 goals

JOHNNY BROWN
1963/64 – 1967/68
175 games, 34 goals

ANDY COLLETT
1994/95 – 1998/99
126 games, 0 goals

LEE ARCHER
1991/92 – 1996/97
126 (25) games, 19 goals

TREVOR CHALLIS
1998/99 – 2002/03
163 (9) games, 1 goal

GRAHAM DAY
1974/75 – 1978/79
146 (1) games, 1 goal

STEWART BARROWCLOUGH
1979/80 – 1980/81
71 (1) games, 17 goals

JUSTIN CHANNING
1992/93 – 1995/96
141 (11) games, 10 goals

CRAIG DISLEY
2004/05 –
24 (11) games, 5 goals

BRIAN BUSH
1947/48 – 1954/55
123 games, 20 goals

BILLY CLARK
1987/88 – 1996/97
273 (17) games, 16 goals

STEVE FOSTER
1997/98 – 2001/02
231 (4) games, 7 goals

BOBBY GOULD
1977/78 – 1978/79
39 (1) games, 13 goals

TREVOR JACOBS
1973/74 – 1975/76
91 games, 3 goals

MATT LOCKWOOD
1996/97 – 1997/98
70 (8) games, 1 goal

MIKE GREEN
1971/72 – 1973/74
89 (3) games, 2 goals

BRYN JONES
1969/70 – 1974/75
96 (10) games, 6 goals

WALLY McARTHUR
1932/33 – 1949/50
280 games, 19 goals

ANDY GURNEY
1993/94 – 1996/97
127 (8) games, 10 goals

GWYN JONES
1962/63 – 1965/66
172 games, 0 goals

AIDEN McCAFFREY
1980/81 – 1984/85
218 (1) games, 12 goals

TERRY HIBBITT
1986/87 – 1988/89
62 (2) games, 5 goals

PHIL KITE
1980/81 – 1983/84
118 games, 0 goals

BARRIE MEYER
1950/51 – 1957/58
143 games, 62 goals

ALEX MUNRO
1962/63 – 1970/71
174 (11) games, 12 goals

TONY POUNDER
1990/91 – 1993/94
114 (12) games, 12 goals

BILL ROOST
1948/49 – 1956/57
198 games, 52 goals

MALCOLM NORMAN
1958/59 – 1961/62
73 games, 0 goals

TONY PULIS
1975/76 – 1983/84
142 (8) games, 5 goals

JOHN RUDGE
1971/72 – 1974/75
56 (22) games, 20 goals

TERRY OLDFIELD
1960/61 – 1965/66
144 (1) games, 11 goals

DAVID PYLE
1956/57 – 1961/62
154 games, 0 goals

JOHN SCALES
1985/86 – 1986/87
80 (5) games, 2 goals

TIM PARKIN
1981/82 – 1985/86
243 (1) games, 14 goals

HOWARD RADFORD
1951/52 – 1961/62
258 games, 0 goals

JUSTIN SKINNER
1991/92 – 1997/98
207 (16) games, 14 goals

TOM STANTON
1968/69 – 1975/76
186 (14) games, 9 goals

NORMAN SYKES
1956/57 – 1963/64
236 games, 10 goals

ANDY THOMSON
1998/99 – 2001/02
143 (3) games, 6 goals

DAVE STANIFORTH
1973/74 – 1978/79
152 (19) games, 34 goals

NICKY TANNER
1985/86 – 1987/88
124 (3) games, 3 goals

JACK WEARE
1946/47 – 1949/50
147 games, 0 goals

WORRALL STERLING
1993/94 – 1995/96
145 (2) games, 7 goals

GARETH TAYLOR
1991/92 – 1995/96
40 (18) games, 16 goals

BRIAN WILLIAMS
1981/82 – 1984/85
201 games, 24 goals

DAVE STONE
1962/63 – 1967/68
162 (4) games, 8 goals

JOHN TAYLOR
1991/92 – 1993/94
103 (4) games, 45 goals

JOHNNY WILLIAMS
1966/67 – 1968/69
73 (4) games, 11 goals

In the Dug-Out

The Post-War Managers

Brough Fletcher 1938 – 1949

Bert Tann 1950 – 1968 (general manager to 1972)

Fred Ford 1968 – 1969

Bill Dodgin Snr 1969 – 1972

Don Megson 1972 – 1977

Bobby Campbell 1978 – 1979

Harold Jarman 1979 – 1980

Terry Cooper 1980 – 1981

Bobby Gould 1981 – 1983

David Williams 1983 – 1985

Bobby Gould 1985 – 1987

Gerry Francis 1987 – 1991

Martin Dobson 1991

Dennis Rofe 1992

Malcolm Allison 1992 – 1993

John Ward 1993 – 1996

Ian Holloway 1996 – 2001

Garry Thompson 2001

Gerry Francis 2001

Garry Thompson 2001 – 2002

Ray Graydon 2002 – 2004

Ian Atkins 2004 –

Fred Ford

Bert Tann

Bill Dodgin Snr

Don Megson

Bobby Campbell

Gerry Francis

THE WINNING FANS

The **Bristol Evening Post** offered its readers a unique chance to get involved with this second edition of **Bristol Rovers Greats**.

The newspaper, which supplied many of the photographs in the book, invited Bristol football fans to nominate the one player they reckoned was most deserving of a place in our updated hall of fame.

The idea was to find out who was the most popular Pirate of the last 15 years, and the people who matter the most have voted by a convincing margin for prolific marksman Marcus Stewart, though it must be admitted that the poll was completed before his recent switch to another local club!

The supporter who gave the best reason for his or her selection, in no more than 20 words, was promised inclusion in the book, together with a free copy of the publication.

The winner is **David Russell** of Hengrove, who wrote: 'Marcus has scored at all levels throughout his career. He is a natural finisher and is still scoring now.'

Runners-up, who also receive **Bristol Rovers Greats**, are **David Hewett** of Stapleton, **Richard Laasna** of Fishponds, and **Leanne Ford** of Whitchurch.

L

B

BANK Cash Cheques.